Quiet Moments

Encouragement for *Daily Living*

KARLENE MILLWOOD

QUIET MOMENTS
ENCOURAGEMENT FOR DAILY LIVING

Unless otherwise indicated, all Scripture quotations are taken from the Holy Bible, New Living Translation, copyright © 1996, 2004, 2007, 2013, 2015 by Tyndale House Foundation. Used by permission of Tyndale House Publishers, Inc., Carol Stream, Illinois 60188. All rights reserved.

Scripture quotations marked KJV are from the Holy Bible, King James Version (Authorized Version). First published in 1611. Quoted from the KJV Classic Reference Bible, Copyright © 1983 by The Zondervan Corporation.

Scripture quotations marked "NCV" are taken from the New Century Version, Copyright © 1987, 1988, 1991 by Word Publishing, a division of Thomas Nelson, Inc. Used by permission. All rights reserved.

Scripture quotations marked AMP are from The Amplified Bible, Old Testament copyright © 1965, 1987 by the Zondervan Corporation. The Amplified Bible, New Testament copyright © 1954, 1958, 1987 by The Lockman Foundation. Used by permission. All rights reserved.

Scripture quotations marked TLB are taken from The Living Bible copyright © 1971. Used by permission of Tyndale House Publishers, Inc., Carol Stream, Illinois 60188. All rights reserved.

Scripture quotations marked MSG are taken from THE MESSAGE. Copyright © 1993, 1994, 1995, 1996, 2000, 2001, 2002, 2003 by Eugene H. Peterson. Used by permission of NavPress Publishing Group. Website.

Scripture quotations marked NASB are taken from the New American Standard Bible®, Copyright © 1960, 1962, 1963, 1968, 1971, 1972, 1973, 1975, 1977, 1995 by The Lockman Foundation. Used by permission.

iUniverse books may be ordered through booksellers or by contacting:

iUniverse
1663 Liberty Drive
Bloomington, IN 47403
www.iuniverse.com
1-800-Authors (1-800-288-4677)

Because of the dynamic nature of the Internet, any web addresses or links contained in this book may have changed since publication and may no longer be valid. The views expressed in this work are solely those of the author and do not necessarily reflect the views of the publisher, and the publisher hereby disclaims any responsibility for them.

Any people depicted in stock imagery provided by Thinkstock are models, and such images are being used for illustrative purposes only. Certain stock imagery © Thinkstock.

ISBN: 978-1-5320-2311-8 (sc)
ISBN: 978-1-5320-2310-1 (e)

Library of Congress Control Number: 2017909066

Print information available on the last page.

iUniverse rev. date: 06/13/2017

Dedication

*To all those who were instrumental in pushing me out
of my comfort zone into the next level*

Contents

Foreword

For thus said the Lord God, the Holy One of Israel: In returning
to Me and resting in Me you shall be saved; in quietness
and in trusting confidence shall be your strength...
[Isaiah 30:15 AMPC]

In today's world, the rapid advancement of technology both connects us and divides us. It makes our lives simpler and, at the same time, more complex. Some elements in the world seek our attention. Some seek our intellectual or emotional engagement. Some, like social media, seek a platform for unfiltered opinions under the guise of truth or an unlocked gateway to relationships. In the end, though, what we really get is simply more noise that intrudes upon our already stressful lives and makes us less able to quiet ourselves when we need quiet most.

In order to free ourselves from stress, fear and worry to have that peace of mind and be in control as we ought in Christ, we must embrace a quiet moment each day, ideally at its start. We must ensure that we consciously and on purpose acknowledge our God and Heavenly Father. We must be in agreement with Him that He made the day; that within each day He has a plan and purpose for our lives; and that He has given us sufficient grace to enable us to do what needs to be done.

That is why this devotional is so timely. In a very noisy world, it reminds us all that quiet moments with God is what truly matters and what makes life within each day count, whether it's Adam in the cool of day in the Garden of Eden, Jesus exemplifying these moments while here on earth, or John on the Island of Patmos. We, too, must recapture what it means to have quiet moments with God, our Father.

For the past six years, I have watched the spiritual growth of the author, Karlene Millwood, and experienced first-hand her commitment to learning how to tap into the ways of the Spirit, which you will experience when you read this devotional. What I most love about the book is the simple yet profoundly life-changing way in which the word is presented and, in particular, the "Meditation" at the end of each chapter that will seal it in your heart.

Apostle Ralph 'Bobby' Somers
Kingdom of Heaven Embassy Ministries

Foreword

As the complexities of this age bear down on humanity, we are seeking different ways to endure the challenges of our everyday lives. Women often become overwhelmed with the task of being wives, mothers, students, employees and leaders in varying sectors of our society.

They are responsible for caring for, and establishing the value systems for the success of their children and generations to come. These responsibilities can demand so much of the giver's time that they can easily lose themselves in their services to others, and forget the importance of spending time with the Lord.

The creator, who holds our being together and causes us to function in wisdom, knowledge and understanding, takes pleasure in our time spent in His word and prayer on a daily schedule. This allows us to hear his will for our lives through his words, gives us the opportunity to speak to him in prayer and to pour out our love, appreciation and thankfulness for all that he has done for us.

For many years, I have practiced spending quiet time with God each day. It is during these times of devotion that I have felt his heart of love, his hands of comfort and his voice of direction.

Thou will show me the path of life; in thy presence there is fullness of joy; at thy right hand there are pleasures for evermore. (Psalm 16:11 KJV).

My admiration and support goes to my sister in the Lord; Karlene Millwood, for introducing this devotional to all women of faith. May each mother, wife, daughter or sister be drawn into a deeper relationship with the Lord. May each moment spent in reading and applying the principles of this devotional become seeds producing a harvest of healing to....... body, soul and spirit.

Bishop Fern B. Mclean
Church of The Living God Int'l.

Preface

M any inspirational books have been written for, and about, women. Quiet Moments devotional has joined this distinguished rank in providing material that will inspire and hopefully motivate Christian women to carve out quiet moments everyday to tap into Divine power and strengthen their walk of faith.

The contents of this book are based on my own experiences and meditations that I journaled over a six year period from 2011 to 2016. Whether it was a morning meditation to start the day, or reflections in the night before going to sleep, I was able to draw spiritual inferences from every facet of my life, be it tending to my plants or watching a television program.

The word of God began to take on more meaning for me through these simple exposures. During this six year period, I had the distinct privilege of leading two womens' groups and became aware of the need for mentoring on how to practically apply the scriptures to everyday life and began to teach what I was learning and experiencing. Instead of teaching merely from intellect, I was able to teach from a place of understanding and experience and connect with their hearts (or spirits) and not just with their minds.

We understand the scriptures and know how to quote them, but the life application is missing when dealing with difficult situations. I prayed and asked the Lord to show me how to apply His word to my life every day. I documented the results of that journey in my journal, and have now transcribed them in the ensuing chapters of this book. I did not study theology, therefore the insights in this book are based solely on my personal journey with the Lord. I am taught by the ultimate teacher; the Holy Spirit.

I will instruct you and teach you in the way you should go; I will counsel you with my loving eye on you. (Psalm 32:8 NIV).

This book, which was drafted during the quiet moments of my one year sabbatical, has been a labour of love, and I would like to say thank you to all those who came alongside to support and encourage me throughout the process.

A special thanks to my own pastor, Ralph (Bobby) Somers, who so graciously and eagerly wrote the foreword. His teaching and mentorship over the years have contributed significantly to the insights reflected in this book. Sincere thanks to Pastor Fern McLean, a woman of God, for her continued encouragement and support of this project. To all those who read, reviewed and endorsed the chapters, I say thank you. I could not have done it without your honesty, insight and love. Thank you all for standing with me and encouraging me.

The chapters are best digested as a devotional in your private moments with God. You will need paper and a pen to answer the questions at the end of each chapter. I hope you will be blessed by the contents of the book. Be encouraged that you are not alone on this journey. From my experiences you will note that you will make many mistakes, fall and get up again, each time stronger than before. That's the journey of life. It's a process. Walk it out.

My love to you all.

Karlene Millwood

...It is in the quiet that we are replenished, renewed and recharged for the demands of our lives. In silence we can reconnect with our true source of energy and inner wisdom. The "still small voice" is heard more in the silence beyond, around and beneath language than it is in the cacophony of incessant sound.
(Sue Patton Thoele)

What Readers Are Saying...

'Quiet Moments' is truly representative of its name. This book is packed with powerful takeaways to meditate upon and also to apply to life. The chapter titled Desperation resonates with me. The one on Intrinsic Value is profound as knowing your worth and value in the Father is essential to self-realization.

'Quiet Moments' can only be expressed as vulnerable and relatable, as it has shown me that growth stems greatly from acceptance of, and learning from, ones failures.

(Novelette M.)

I like that the author uses her personal experiences to highlight the different lessons. The reader is able to relate based on similar experiences or challenges. The chapter that spoke about humility helped me to change my perception of an individual and as a result, I was able to enjoy interacting with the person, where I wasn't able to before. It was a great read, and one that I will continually read.

(Kareen G.)

This is a very good devotional. It is such a timely reminder of God's great love for us. The Intrinsic Value chapter reminded me of what's most important in life. This devotional ministers to me and challenges me to live an empowering and Godly life. Love it!

(Camise B.)

This work is truly well thought out and speaks from a real relationship with the Father. It makes one think, because it is relatable. The meditations/ reflections enables the reader to really digest the chapters. Sing, O Barren Woman, spoke volumes to me. Even the title reminded me to worship in the waiting process. It corrected me to celebrate the precious gifts He has given me. Simply wonderful work.

(Tania C.)

1 The Importance of Living by God's Word

I like flowers. I have so many potted plants in my house because I believe that they add beauty and ambience to any space. Plus it is good for the oxygen-carbohydrate exchange which we need to live. I have been planting flowers since I was a teenager and living with my grandmother in the Caribbean.

What I have noticed about these plants is that they need a few things to grow. Most importantly are healthy soil and water. If I should uproot any of these plants and leave them out of the soil, they would eventually die because they have been removed from their natural environment. Without the soil to provide nutrients for the roots, the plants' growth would be affected even if I continued to water it constantly.

Every living organism needs the right environment to grow. Fish and amphibians need water, birds need the open air, trees and flowers need healthy soil. Every living thing has its own environment in which it thrives. When it is disturbed, they begin to die.

So it is with humanity. When God created man (humanity or mankind) He took us out of Himself, the Source of all life. God is a Spirit, so if He took us out of Himself it means we were first spirit. He fashioned a body for us and placed us on the earth. The earth is not our natural habitat even though God created it for us. We came from somewhere and was placed on the earth. We came out of the creator.

Therefore in order for us to thrive, we must stay within our natural, healthy habitat - in God. When Eve was deceived by the serpent and got her husband Adam to join her, sin entered and they were cut off from their natural environment. Sin rooted them up out of the soil of the Spirit of God, and as a result they died spiritually and set humanity on that downward spiral.

God, in His wisdom, loved us so much that He put insurance in place to make a way for us to be re-introduced to our natural habitat. He sent His son to earth in the form of a human, to die for our redemption. This wonderful act is summed up nicely in the gospels but for this I will use John chapter one.

Before the world began, the Word was there. The Word was with God, and the Word was God. He was there with God in the beginning. Everything was made through Him, and nothing was made without Him. (John 1:1-3 ERV).

God's Word framed creation. Faith helps us to understand that God created the whole world by His command. This means that the things we see were made by something that cannot be seen. (Hebrews 11:3 ERV)

God's word has been around from the beginning. He gave us His Word in scriptures to help us live abundantly in the earth. Solomon told us in the book of Proverbs, *"The words are the secret to life and health to all who discover them."* (Proverbs 4:22 ERV)

When we choose to live by the Word of God it nourishes us and gives us life. We are infused by the very Spirit of God as we meditate His word. Rightly applying what we have learned to the situations in our lives, guarantees us victory every time.

God's word is also protection from the onslaught of the enemy. God is one with His word. His word is spirit and life. (John 6:63). God is His word as we saw in the first few verses of John chapter one. When we live according to the Word, we are covered, hidden, surrounded by God.

His Word is our shield, defense, and protection against the lies, deception and attacks of the enemy. Living in His word is living in Him. Attacks and criticisms cannot affect us when we are under God's covering.

It is very important to make time every day to read and meditate on God's Word. It is the very essence of life.

Always remember what is written in that book of law. Speak about that book and study it day and night. Then you can be sure to obey what is written there. If you do this, you will be wise and successful in everything you do. (Joshua 1:8 ERV).

1.1   Meditation

References: John 1:1-3, 6:23; Hebrews 11:3; Proverbs 4:22; Joshua 1:8

1.   What stands out for you in this lesson?

2.   How important is God's Word to humanity?

3.   How important is God's word to the church?

4.   How important is God's word to you personally?

5.   Besides the scriptures above, find two others that talk about the importance of living by God's Word.

6.   How did you apply the Word to your life today? (Give a situation)

2   Desperation

A while back when I was still working in the corporate world, I planned my day out nicely. I knew exactly how I wanted to spend those most important waking hours, trying to make every moment count.

I had planned to use my lunch break to go to the store run some errands, but incidentally my morning was dragging on a bit, so I took the liberty to run the errands a little earlier on my morning break instead.

I stepped outside into the blustering cold of the winter morning. Every bone in my body was telling me to go back inside but I decided to press on and get this over with.

Twice I felt like turning back. Not only was it cold, but I was also feeling a stabbing pain in both my heels. I continued on despite the pain because something kept telling me to just go, so I slowly walked the half block. As I was crossing the street I vaguely heard a woman's voice. She was coming up the street toward me.

Everyone she approached ignored and passed her by like she was invisible. She caught up with me just before I entered the store. She spoke to me in her halting English, "Please...help me buy breakfast. I'm hungry."

"I'm sorry. I don't have any money," I told her.

The woman insisted, "Please, I'm hungry. Just help me get something to eat." I sighed as she continued, "Miss, I'm cold and I'm hungry. I slept outside last night. Please help me!"

I looked at her as she spoke trying to spot any signs of lying. Let's face it. As much as we want to help every time a homeless person asks, we are skeptical to do so sometimes. I know I am. Not because I am mean or stingy. Far from it, but some of them lie blatantly about what they are going to do with the money. They use it to buy drugs, alcohol or cigarettes.

So even though I felt compassion for her I hesitated. I was also concerned about her so I continued the conversation.

"Where did you sleep?" I engaged her further in conversation.

"In the stairwell of a building," she replied.

Her teeth were brown and rotting and as we talked all sorts of thoughts were going through my mind. She interrupted my thoughts.

"Miss, please. Help me. I just want to go to McDonald's or somewhere around here and buy something to eat."

I looked up the street to where McDonald's was. My thought was to take her there and buy her the food instead of giving her the money, which wasn't mine to give anyway. I remembered that my feet were hurting and I didn't want to walk more than I had to.

While I deliberated on whether I should give her the fifteen dollars or not, she suddenly fell to her knee on the cold sidewalk with her hands clasped and stretched out to me.

"Please help me."

"No, don't do that!" I said, quickly reaching down to help her stand up.

Without another thought I reached into my purse and gave her the fifteen dollars that I was holding for a friend.

"Thank you. Thank you."

"Don't spend it all at once. Leave some for lunch," I told her. She thanked me again and walked away fumbling to put the money in her handbag.

I pushed the door to go into the store and turned around in time to see her going into the 7-11. My last thought about the encounter was, "God I leave it in your hands. I gave to meet a need but if she uses it otherwise, it's in your hands."

I thought about the Siro-Phoenician woman who went to Jesus to ask Him to pray for her demon-possessed daughter. Jesus tried to discourage her and even called her a dog, but that didn't stop her. She did to Jesus exactly what this woman did to me; she knelt in front of Him and kept on asking.

Just as Jesus was moved to grant her request as a result of her desperation, so I was moved to help this woman. If it is normal for us humans to show mercy in the face of another's desperation, how much more our Heavenly Father?

Scripture abounds with stories of people who went desperate before God and had their prayers answered; Hannah, Hezekiah, Blind Bartimaeus, the woman with the issue of blood and the list goes on.

It left me to ask these questions:

1. How do I go to God when I am facing an impossible situation?
2. Do I relentlessly apply faith for my answer, or do I pray pitiful prayers?

His Word says, *And so I tell you, keep on asking you will receive what you ask for. Keep on seeking, and you will find. Keep on knocking, and the door will be opened to you.* (Luke 11:9 NLT).

Hebrews 11:6 says He rewards those who diligently seek Him. This woman was a diligent seeker. It was an eye opener to me that desperation commands an immediate response. If I could respond instantly to this woman when she knelt in front of me, how much more will God respond when we worship him? How much more will He respond to my persistent, diligent, desperate faith?

Three things became clear to me that day:

1. It was a clear demonstration that faith requires persistent, diligent, doggedness.
2. The Lord responds to sincere worship.
3. Desperation will always evoke an act of mercy.

We shouldn't only go desperate to God when we want something from Him. We should also be desperate for Him. Even more so.

Isaiah exhorts us in chapter fifty five verse six (ERV), *"So you should look for the Lord before it is too late. You should call Him now, while He is near."*

When we go to Him desperate for Him, He rewards us by blanketing us in His holy presence. What more could you ask for?

Are you desperate for God? Are you seeking Him daily?

2.1 Meditation

References: Luke 11:9, Isaiah 55:6

1. What stands out for you in this lesson?

2. What comes to mind when you hear the word desperate?

3. Name two persons in scripture who prayed desperately to God. Provide scriptures.

4. Have you ever gone to God in desperation? If yes, what was the end result?

5. Describe a time when you responded mercifully to someone's desperate need?

6. What should we be most desperate for?

7. Are you?

3 | Intrinsic Value

I remember it like it was yesterday. October 15, 2013. The day the Holy Spirit reminded me about my worth (value). I was going about my day as usual when I noticed that two words were playing over and over and over again in my mind. Intrinsic Value.

Of course, I was a little puzzled as to why I was thinking about them. I didn't hear them or read them anywhere, so where did they come from and why? I didn't immediately understand why so I prayed about it and made a note in my journal.

Although I had an understanding of what intrinsic value meant, I still decided to look up the words in the dictionary for a clearer definition. This is what I found:

Intrinsic: Belonging to a thing by its very nature.
Belonging to or lying within a given part; Native, innate, natural, true, real.

Value: Worth, power, purpose, quality, significance, substance, superiority, advantage, force.
The worth of something in comparison to things for which it can be exchanged.

Later that night in our Bible study, the Holy Spirit brought further revelation through our pastor. He said, "My worth *(value)* is nothing. Jesus gives me strength, *(power, force, ability, substance)* to do everything." (Parentheses mine). In other words, of myself I am nothing. Whatever value I have comes from Christ and His nature and ability in me.

Our worth does not come from things like nice cars, big houses, titles or lots of money. It doesn't come from what people think or say about us, the type of job we do, or how many degrees we have. Not that it's wrong to have any of these things, however we should recognize and acknowledge the One who gives us the ability to do or achieve those things. Our true worth comes from knowing God; Who He is to us and in us, and who we are to Him and in Him.

I am a son of God. I am the Righteousness of God. I am seated in Heavenly places in Christ above principalities and powers. I have power to tread upon serpents and scorpions and I shall not be harmed. I have power over every ability of the devil and nothing shall in any wise harm me. (Ephesians 2:6; John 1:12; Luke 10:19). I speak these words over myself often to remind the devil who I am and whose I am. It also reminds me who I am and that I have a big God on my side. So no matter what I face, it cannot diminish my worth.

Some time ago I was dealing with a difficult situation and I cried out to the Lord about it. To be truthful I vented the way I would to a close friend. There were no nice, O Heavenly Fathers or Dear Lords, or any such thing. To be honest, I threw a tantrum. I poured my heart out to God, as David instructed us to do in Psalm 62:8, and then went to bed.

As I was falling asleep I saw a vision of the Lord sitting on the side of my bed. He gently stretched His hand and caressed my forehead, like a loving father would to his child, and whispered, "The Holy Spirit makes it easy."

I jumped up out of my sleep and looked around the bedroom but I was alone (physically). Nevertheless I knew exactly what happened. My Heavenly Father came through the Holy Spirit to comfort me in my time of need, and to remind me who I had working for me. I should trust His ability to get me through.

Two Greek words that are used to describe the Holy Spirit are *Dunamis* and *Parakletos*. *Dunamis* speaks of His ability, while *Parakletos* refers to His function: advocate, adviser, helper – one who is called to one's aid. Both words, though different in definition speak of the divine power of the same

Holy Spirit. To put them in context, when we depend on the *Parakletos*, He gives us *Dunamis* to deal with life situations.

When you understand the Holy Spirit's function in your life, you come to know that you are not at the mercy of any situation because a greater power is at work in you. I approach situations differently as a result of this revelation. *I can do all things through Christ who strengthens me* (Philippians 4:13 KJV), because Jesus gave us all that He is and has. Putting it all in context later on, I came up with this:

I have the superior advantage to do everything because of the substance (power, nature, ability) of Christ in me to strengthen me. My strength comes from confidence of my identity and position in Him, and knowing that I am secure in Him.

This is, and should be, the only thing that our value (worth) rests on. Christ in us. Our value is not determined by what we do as careers, what we drive, where we live, or what people think and say about us. It is solely dependent on who is in us and with us. We make things valuable. Things don't give us value.

The quality of a product is determined by the company that makes it. The quality of the product dictates its worth. The higher the quality the more expensive it is and vice-versa. Where we come from determines our quality (value, worth). We were made in the image (likeness, character) of God.

Then God said, "Let us make human beings in our image, to be like us. (Genesis 1:26a NLT).

My sister, you have value (worth) whether you are rejected or accepted, spoken well of or spoken evil of, understood or misunderstood, raised up or trampled on, celebrated or hated. Nothing or no one can lower your value. You are in the god class. Stand in your intrinsic power!

Doing things in our own strength is difficult and can be futile, but when we know who we are and whose we are, and learn to depend on Christ's power in us, it becomes easy to handle any situation. Know your worth.

3.1 Meditation

References: Philippians 4:13; Ephesians 2:6; John 1:12; Luke 10:19; Psalm 62; Genesis 1:26

1. What stands out for you in this lesson?

2. Describe Intrinsic Value in your own words.

3. What does it mean to depend on the Holy Spirit?

4. Have you discovered and are you confident about your intrinsic value?

5. What determines your worth?

6. Who are you and whose are you?

7. Define the words Dunamis and Parakletos and use each in a sentence.

4 Identity Crisis

T he month of May is designated as Child Month in certain countries. I think of the parenting methods of many parents today and I feel sad sometimes that in the twenty-first century there are still so many archaic mindsets about how to raise children.

It irks me when I hear people say to children, "Why can't you be like [insert name here]? These are five of the most dangerous words a parent could utter to a child. Those words can be like a dagger that pierces and kills the soul in a slow, painful death. It's like being cut with a razor and being left to bleed out slowly.

What the parent unknowingly does with those words is tell the child that he or she is not enough; he or she is inadequate, something is wrong with who they are and they need to become like the *person of choice* in order to be accepted.

That wound to the soul can be fatal if it is not healed in a healthy, loving way. If this is not corrected early, the child will grow up with an inferiority complex and feel insecure about who they are. An insecure person may operate from one of two extremes:

1. They become timid, shy and may shut down their creativity which could derail them from reaching their full potential.
2. Or they may go to the other extreme of becoming over achievers, forever trying to please the person who wound them subconsciously.

This constant need to achieve can become an addiction, and they go through life never attaining that sense of adequacy that they are pursuing. In the world people perform to be accepted, but in the Kingdom of God, we are accepted because we are His sons. (John 1:12).

Individuals who find themselves in this performance dilemma tend never to have a strong sense of self. They don't know who they are or who they are supposed to be and constantly try to prove themselves to be accepted.

They go through life taking on different personas; imitating people that they think are cool, or that they admire. It all boils down to trying to measure up. In pursuing this false identity they lose all sense of self and that can be worse than death. They become the living dead; alive but not really there, i.e the REAL them is not known.

That subtle form of abuse is injurious to a human being. To take away one's sense of self or to subdue the individual's personality is an insult to them and their Creator. To treat a person in this manner is to intimate that God made a mistake in how He created them. This suppression robs them of the most valuable thing they can possess – their God-given identity. Knowing who we are is the beginning of the roadmap of our lives.

King David got a revelation of how special he was. He came to realize that when God made him, He created a masterpiece. He said, *"You made all the delicate, inner parts of my body and knit me together in my mother's womb. Thank you for making me so wonderfully complex! Your workmanship is marvelous – how well I know it."* (Psalm 139:13-14 NLT). That scripture applies to you as much as it applied to David. Take those words and apply them to yourself and realize what a masterpiece you are.

In the movie Avatar, the natives of the planet Pandora greet each other by saying, "I see you." This goes beyond seeing them in the physical and delves into the essence of who the person is. It validates the individual and gives the feeling that *you are important to me*. It is difficult to mistreat or abnormally use (abuse) someone that we *see*. To see is to know, to understand. Understanding comes through knowledge. Therefore to see a person is to know him or her – ascribing importance, worthiness and value.

We were each created with a purpose, to fulfill a destiny, something specific, in this lifetime. (Jeremiah 1:5). Only when we know who we are can we discover what we are supposed to do. As discussed elsewhere in this book, doing comes out of being. So to take away or subdue someone's sense of self is to rob them of purpose.

You may as well take away their breath because, until they find purpose, they will only be wandering through the wilderness of life, going from one dry place to another hallucinating about oases. They will never end up in that lush, fruitful land that was destined for them before the creation. Yes. Before creation. So parents, be careful of the words you speak to your children. Be careful of what you are releasing over their lives. Words are powerful and they have creative ability. Say what you want to see.

If you, as an adult, have experienced and are still struggling with this, get in the Presence of God and let Him heal you. Your identity is found in Him alone, and you should seek to please Him alone, and measure up only to His standards (Word).

Then God said, "Let us make a man—someone like ourselves (Genesis 1:26a TLB). When God created man He took man out of Himself. Adam and Eve fell and caused a separation from God, but the second Adam came to restore that connection. (1 Corinthians 15:21-22).

If you are a believer in Christ, your spirit has been redeemed and your connection to your Source has been re-established. So no need to try to be like anyone else, you are already like God. Find your identity in Him. *For in Him you live, move and have your being. (Acts 17:28 KJV).*

4.1 Meditation

References: Jeremiah 1:5; Job 22:28

1. What stood out for you in this lesson?

2. What does the scripture say about raising children?

3. Why is it important to speak the Word of God over our children, and ourselves?

4. What does it mean to SEE someone?

5. Why is it sometimes dangerous to imitate other people?

6. Where should you find your identity? List scriptures that speak of this.

7. What does it mean to be God's masterpiece?

5   Those Little Frustrations

L ife gives us many reasons to become frustrated. I can remember a point in my life where it seemed like the only emotion I had was frustration. So many things were happening and I couldn't catch a break. I was easily irritated and snapped at people in a flash. Frustrations show up to teach us important lessons. It is up to us to learn and grow from them, so that when similar situations show up we will respond differently.

During those times of frustration it didn't take much to set me off. Some days I felt like just packing my things and leaving and not letting anyone know where I was. I would just vanish and never return, but I asked myself what purpose would that serve? So I humbled myself and I kept on going, kept on praying and asking God for grace to get through.

I had to rely on the Holy Spirit a lot to get me through those trials. I know I had to refrain from saying or doing anything about the situation and just leave it to the Lord, because He told me this in a vision a couple weeks prior to it all. This is where the Lord's strength was manifest. It is only Him that kept me from doing all the foolish things I wanted to do. What I didn't realize at that time is that in the crucible of these trials I was being changed.

Lisa Bevere said in her book, *Without Rival*, "God uses outward pressure in our lives to produce the inward transformation that prepares us for our destiny."

The Potter had me on His spinning wheel and he was using these situations to mold and shape me into who He wants me to be. Have you ever seen anyone make pottery? The potter gets the wheel spinning rapidly, then he plops a piece of unformed clay on top of it and begins to shape it with his hands. He constantly puts water on the clay to keep it malleable. As the wheel is rapidly spinning, the potter is busy forming that piece of clay into his desired shape for it.

The only thing keeping the clay from flying off the wheel is the potter's hands. When the potter is satisfied with the shape of the clay, he stops the wheel and allows the clay to dry. Only after that piece of clay has attained the potters desired form does he stop the process. If there is a tiny little abnormality he molds it right out until he has perfection, unless he purposefully intended it to have a glitch in the design.

That is how God molds us into His image. He will not stop until every spot and wrinkle is out of us. He will continue to mold and shape us into what we were created to be, and He will use these frustrations as tools in his molding process. We just have to remain malleable in His hands.

In the book of Jeremiah, the Lord used the prophet to warn rebellious Israel about the coming judgement for their idolatrous ways. In chapter eighteen the Lord sent Jeremiah to the potters shop to wait for instructions from Him. From verse four the prophet recounted what he saw.

But the jar he (the potter) was making did not turn out as he had hoped, so he crushed it into a lump of clay again and started over. Then the Lord gave me this message: O Israel, can I not do to you as this potter has done to his clay? As the clay is in the potter's hand, so are you in my hand. (Parentheses mine). (Jeremiah 18:4-6 NLT).

His spinning wheel is the life challenges that we face - the frustrations, the hurts, the betrayals and the rejections. He has a purpose for them all. Allow Him to continue to pour His Spirit (water) upon you. It will soften you up and make you more pliable – easier to shape.

The next time you are faced with a frustrating situation, remember that the Lord is working in you to do His good pleasure. (Philippians 2:13 KJV). Instead of waiting for the situation to change, ask God to change you from within.

Charis Hillman-Brown wrote, "The gift in frustration is that, had we never been aggravated, we would never have been uncomfortable enough to even think about trying to change what bothers us. Perhaps we must first be willing to change ourselves."

You will begin to look at the situation through His eyes, handle it correctly with His help, and be better equipped to change what is causing the frustration. I pray for you that as He did in me, He will do the same in you.

May he equip you with all you need for doing His will. May He produce in you, through the power of Jesus Christ, every good thing that is pleasing to Him. (Hebrews 13:21 NLT). In Jesus' Name. Amen.

5.1 Meditation

References: Jeremiah 18:4-6; Philippians 2:13; Hebrews 13:21

1. What stands out for you in this lesson?

2. When faced with frustration, how do you handle it?

3. Describe the similarities of God's molding process with pottery making.

4. List at least two other scriptures that you would use to help with overcoming feelings of frustration.

5. When you feel frustrated, what needs to change? Why?

6 Idols

One night while worshipping an image of a cow's head with a golden nose invaded my mind. I prayed and spoke against it thinking it was demonic, but when it wouldn't go away I stopped. The Holy Spirit helped me understand that it is a golden calf; an idol. I had idols in my life. There were things that I was putting before Him.

I repented immediately, but I was very shaken by the revelation. It made me go back to read Exodus 32 where Aaron made the golden calf for the Israelites to worship. As I read a few things jumped out at me:

1.   When the people saw that Moses took so long to come down from the mountain where he went to meet with God they gave up hope. Moses did not return in the time they expected and that made them feel deserted. They felt abandoned and sought a substitute.

     I began to look into my life to see where I may have been substituting anything for God. Could it be that I was using things that I was doing at that time as substitutes for the lack of progress in my spiritual life. Was I using them to fill a void because the breakthroughs that I was expecting were too long in coming?

     I looked around me and others seemed to be growing and being promoted and I didn't seem to be moving. I believe I was in the will of God with the projects I was working on, but in the process may have started to put too much emphasis on them.

2.   The people took off their gold jewelry and gave it to Aaron who made it into an idol for them to worship.

They made a god out of what they had. Instead of continuing to wait for Moses to return to hear what God had to say, they made themselves a god. It is important to wait on God's timing. When we move without Him we are likely to fall into the same trap – making gods out of the things we pursue or have. When we wait on Him and seek Him first then He will give us what we need.

In her devotional, Joyce Meyer confirmed this to me that very day. She wrote, "In our impatience, we often take matters into our own hands. I say we get "bright ideas" – plans of our own, which we hope God will bless. These plans open the door for confusion and chaos. Then their results must be dealt with, which often delays our miracle."

3. It is easy to drift away from God in a time of waiting.

    When Moses came down from Sinai...he saw the wickedness of the Israelites who had become impatient in waiting. He became angry and broke the tablets on which the Ten Commandments were written. Sometimes waiting is the best thing for us because it helps develop the character of God in us, and brings us to a place where we seek only His will for what we should be doing.

    I love how Os Hillman said it in his devotional, *His Vision, His Way, In His Timing.* "God often births a vision in our lives only to allow it to die first before the purest version of the vision is manifested. When God gives a vision and darkness follows, waiting on God will bring you into accordance with the vision if you await His timing. If not, you try to do away with the supernatural in God's undertakings. Never try to help God fulfill His word."

    As I continued praying and listening to God that morning he gave me another vision of a covered pot on a stove. It had steam coming out of it indicating that it was boiling. The words SPIRIT OF THE LORD floated above the pot. They seemed to be hanging off the light fixture above the stove.

    The prophet Jeremiah also saw a boiling pot – his was tilting from the North. Jeremiah 1:16-17 NIV God says, *"I will pronounce my judgement on my people because of their wickedness in forsaking me, in burning incense to other gods and in worshipping what their hands have made."*

All throughout the book of Jeremiah, God used the prophet to chastise Israel for their adulterous ways in turning away again to worship idols.

Moses handled the idol worshipping situation decisively. He stood at the entrance to the camp and called out, *"All who are on the Lord's side, come here and join me."* (Exodus 32:26 NLT).

When the Levites joined him he commanded them to take their swords and carry out the judgement that the Lord commanded. The Levites went back and forth with their swords that day, slaughtering as much as three thousand people. (Exodus 32: 27-28 NLT). While God no longer sanctions this mode of punishment, we are still required to revere Him alone as God. He is holy and He is sovereign. Therefore we should never put anything or anyone before Him. He alone deserves our worship and our praise. Ask God to help you identify any idols in your life.

6.1 Meditation

References: Exodus 32; Jeremiah 1:13-16

1. What stood out for you in this lesson?

2. According to the scripture what is idolatry? List relevant scriptures.

3. What is an idol?

4. How did God deal with idol worshippers in the Old Testament?

5. How does he deal with them today?

6. From studying this lesson, can you identify any idols in your life?

7. Would you be able to tell if there were idols in your life?

7   The Secret Place

I read Psalm 91 in the *Amplified Bible* before going to bed one night and the Holy Spirit began to unpack it for me. The song was in my mind earlier and I followed up with reading the chapter. Better still, He confirmed parts of this revelation to me through my Pastor in our Bible study.

The more I read was the more the revelation came. I felt so alive. Instead of feeling sleepy, I was fully awake. I went to bed very late that night as I allowed the Holy Spirit to minister to me through His word. I am now sharing with you what he revealed to me.

He who dwells (rests, remains, abides) in the secret place of the Most High God,

> No one knows this place except Him. Satan cannot find this place because it is known only to God.

Shall remain stable and fixed under the shadow of the Almighty (whose power no foe can withstand).

> Stable and fixed – *Those who trust in the Lord are steady as Mount Zion, unmoved by any circumstance.* (Psalm 125:1 TLB).

> We are not tossed to and fro like the double minded man who is unstable in all His ways. We are fixed (well-positioned, unmovable) as we remain under the shadow of the God who has all might

(strength) and power in His hands – under the shadow of the unshakable, unchangeable and unbreakable God.

If we are in His shadow He has to be present. What is a shadow except a reflection of a thing in the presence of light? He is the Light, therefore His shadow is a reflection of Himself cast by Himself (the Light). So when I remain under His shadow, I am really abiding in His presence, in Love, in Light in Shadow, or in the Shadow of Light.

Shadows are absent in darkness. Darkness does not cast shadows, they can only be seen in the presence of light. So though I am in a shadow, I have light (clarity, understanding). I am shaded, protected in and with understanding. *His truth and faithfulness are a shield and a buckler* (v4).

When we are in His shadow sometimes we are going to be in front of Him, beside Him or behind Him. In the natural, shadows move based on the position of the light. God, who is light, knows which angle the enemy will attack from so He positions Himself around us strategically so that we remain hidden from the enemy.

If the enemy is trying to attack from behind, He puts His shadow in front and takes up the rear guard. If the enemy is coming from the front He lets the shadow fall behind so He can go ahead and there are times when it is safer to walk beside Him, so that's where the shadow falls.

Whose power no foe can withstand.

The Holy Spirit spoke a word to me a few months ago that fits here perfectly. He said, "The Spirit of the invincible conqueror is in you." I thought about it and realized that nowhere in scripture is it recorded that God ever lost a battle. That is because He is a conqueror and *no foe can withstand His power.* He is invincible. Unstoppable.

I will say of the Lord, He is my refuge and my fortress, my God; on Him I lean and rely, and in Him I [confidently] trust.

When I speak or declare who He is to me, I am activating my faith. Faith speaks. When I declare Him as my Refuge and Fortress (Protection), it moves Him to do exactly what I say of Him. He is moved by faith and responds only to faith. We could move verse 14 up to this point because we clearly see the Lord's response and His action plan as a result of the declaration of faith.

Because he has set his love upon Me, therefore will I deliver him; I will set him on high, because he knows and understands My name [has personal knowledge of My mercy, love and kindness – trusts and relies on Me, knowing I will never forsake him, no, never].

In verse 14 He makes the decision to deliver. He is pleased with the declaration of faith so in verse 15 He makes a promise that when the person of faith calls on Him, He will (most assuredly) answer. He promises to be with him in trouble, adversity, calamity, and to always deliver him out of them.

He promises long life with continuous salvation in the last verse of the chapter, verse 16.

Now let us go back to verse 3. In this verse we see the action plan in verses 14 – 16 carried out.

For then He will deliver you from the snare of the fowler and from the deadly pestilence.

[Then] – meaning as a result of. As a result of activating your faith by speaking the word and declaring who He is to you, He delivers you, but He doesn't just lift you out of the situation and leaves you.

[Then] He will cover you with His pinions, and under His wings shall you trust and find refuge; His truth and His faithfulness are a shield and a buckler.

He covers (hides) you under His wings and feathers. He doesn't leave you out in the open to be susceptible to the enemy's attacks, no, you are covered; hidden in His secret place, where the enemy cannot find you. And because of this –

You do not have to be afraid of the terror of the night (adversity, calamity), nor of the arrow (the evil plots and slanders of the wicked) that flies by day,

Nor of the pestilence and sudden death that surprise and lay waste at noonday.

A thousand may fall at your side, and ten thousand at your right hand, but it shall not come near you. (Parentheses mine).

> Why? Because I am covered, hidden, inaccessible in the secret place. God's covering is like a two way mirror. You can see out but who is outside cannot see in. You can see *everything* that is happening, but the enemy can't see you. This is your ability to discern.

> So he throws darts and arrows to try to get you out of your position in your secure place. As long as you continue to lean and rely and confidently trust in the Lord, you are safe and the enemy cannot affect you, because he cannot find you.

> However if you begin to fear and back down from your faith, it will leave you exposed to the enemy. Fear opens the door for the enemy to find you and defeat you. Satan senses us through fear but when we stand in faith, it shuts the door to fear and connects us with God. That is why you are commanded, "You **shall not** be afraid..." Satan works through fear, so in the absence of fear he has nothing to use against you.

Only a spectator shall you be [yourself inaccessible in the secret place of the Most High] as you witness the reward of the wicked.

Because you have made the Lord your refuge, and the Most High your dwelling place, there shall no evil befall you, nor any plague or calamity come near your tent.

> Evil plagues and calamities cannot find you in the secret place. They will look for you but they will have to pass over you because you are covered, sheltered in the secret place of the Most High. In His Almighty shadow.

In the book of Exodus when Pharaoh continued to harden his heart against God, God sent the plagues to show Pharaoh his power. While Egypt was being inflicted with all these calamities, the Israelites were untouched by them.

One of the most memorable is the angel of death passing through the land and killing the firstborn of every Egyptian household.

For the Lord will pass through to slay the Egyptians; and when He sees the blood upon the lintel [above the entry way] and the two side posts, the Lord will pass over the door and will not allow the destroyer to come into your houses to slay you.

Pharaoh rose up in the night, he, and all his servants, and all the Egyptians; and there was a great cry [of heartache and sorrow] in Egypt, for there was not a house where there was not one dead. (Exodus 12: 23 & 30 AMP).

God is our protector and deliverer. He can be trusted to do what He says. None of those plagues came near the Israelites and Pharaoh had to let them go.

For He will give his angels [especial] charge over you to accompany and defend and preserve you in all your ways [of obedience and service]. They shall bear you up on their hands, lest you dash your foot against a stone.

Psalm 34:7 NLT says, *"For the Angel of the Lord is a guard; he surrounds and defends all who fear Him."*

You are assured of His protection because He assigns a security detail to you. He has taken personal responsibility for your safety. The angel(s) never let you out of their sight. If you stub your toe (figuratively) they are there to catch you. As a matter of fact they won't allow you to stub your toe. They will lift you up over the stone.

Therefore no danger, hazard, obstacle can stop you! Angels are assigned to bear you up over every one. They see the obstacles beforehand and just lifts you up over them. So the very obstacles that were meant to stop you, pushes you higher. The angels lift you up over them – to go up is to rise higher.

You shall tread upon the lion and adder; the young lion and the serpent shall you trample underfoot.

You have authority over demons to tread (trample, crush, bring down) every work of the devil and walk in complete victory.

He shall call upon Me, and I will answer him; I will be with him in trouble, I will deliver him and honor him. With long life will I satisfy him and show him My salvation.

Faith ensures our victory. *For whatever is born of God overcomes the world; and this is the victory that overcomes the world - our faith.* (1 John 4:4 NKJV).

Faith pleases God. That is why He takes no pleasure in those who draw back (Hebrews 10:38 KJV). When you draw back, you are pulling back into enemy territory to walk in fear. He cannot deliver and work for you in that state because you tell the Lord that you don't trust Him. You haven't set your love on him.

Notice what the Lord says in verse 14. *"Because he has set his love on me..."* When we use our faith, we set our love on Him and He is now bound to respond out of who He is. He is love.

If we are in His shadow, He has to be present. Abiding in His shadow is also abiding in His presence – in His love. It's all about love.

God is love. His shadow (reflection) is also love – therefore God's secret place is His love. When we remain (abide) under His shadow, we are abiding in/under His love. Satan cannot love – he doesn't know how. So when you walk in love, we become the Lord's reflection; His shadow. We become the very shadow that we are abiding under. It's like a camouflage.

Soldiers wear camouflage gear into conflict so that they can blend into their terrain. So the Father uses His shadow to camouflage us from the enemy. Satan is looking for you but all he is seeing is God (Love). Satan throws out his ammunition (terrors of the night, arrows, pestilence, destruction and sudden death) to try to flush you out of your hiding place, but all you have to do is abide, abide, abide.

7.1 Meditation

References: Psalm 91, 37:4, 125:1; Hebrews 10:38, 11:6; 1 John 4:4

1. What stood out for you in this lesson?

2. What is God's secret place? Explain.

3. What is a shadow?

4. In your own words, explain what it means to dwell in God's shadow?

5. Faith pleases God. List at least two other things from scripture that pleases God. Provide scriptures.

6. What does God promise to do when we call upon Him?

7. What can God's covering be compared to?

8. What is the purpose of angels? Find at least two other scriptures that tells us their purpose.

9. What is faith, and what is its purpose? Provide scriptures.

10. What is fear, and what is its purpose? Provide scriptures.

8 The Fullness of Who He Is

I woke up one morning to hear my spirit singing the well-known worship song, "This is the Air I Breathe." I got out of bed and joined my mind and body with my spirit in song in worship to the King of Kings. During worship I thanked my Lord for always being with me.

"I don't know how you do it, but you have given ALL of yourself to those who are called by your name. Not just a piece of you, but ALL of you is within each of us." I said to Him.

He responded, "When you obey my word, you will come into the fullness of all that I am."

I never thought of it that way before. God is a Spirit. So are His words. (John 6:63). So when we come into knowledge and understanding of the word, and rightly apply it to our lives, we grow up into (become like) Him.

Man shall not live by bread alone, but by every word that proceeds from the mouth of God. (Matthew 4:4 NKJV).

How can a young person live a clean life? By carefully reading the map of your Word. (Psalm 119:9 (The Message)).

The Heavenly Father speaks to us through His word. Jesus was able to do what He did on earth without sin because He did nothing without hearing from His Father. We see how powerful Jesus' life and ministry was as a result. Christ left His spirit in the earth as our guide to help us grow up into the things of God.

Nelson Mandela was or still is considered a great man. This man saw the people of South Africa suffer so much injustice during Apartheid and took it upon himself to make a difference. This quest for justice cost him dearly.

He spent twenty seven years in jail as a result of going against the system of Apartheid. He triumphed in the end when he was released to become the first black President in that nation of predominantly black people.

Mandela's ideologies remain with us in the earth through our memories of him, however, we will not or cannot grow into the fullness of who he was. We can imitate some things about him but we cannot become fully him. Though he was great, he was flawed.

Mandela's spirit cannot bring us into perfection even though his life has impacted many so powerfully through his forgiveness and reconciliation philosophy. This philosophy (law) is not Mandela's. It is Jesus' law. Forgive your enemies and pray for them. Do good to them that hate you.

So even in his greatness Mandela activated and lived someone else's law. The law of a higher authority. It is his obedience to this higher authority that made him great.

Jesus, on the other hand, obeyed laws that He put in place from creation – His own laws. He is the highest authority. Jesus' spirit is still in the earth. We can come into the fullness of it because we have a manual that teaches us how to do it. Mandela read the manual and we saw the results in his life.

Jesus is great and He is flawless. He is bringing us into perfection through the spirit of His word. His Spirit has the divine power to do that. So as you seek Him and cooperate with His spirit (Word, Manual of Life) you grow into looking like Him more and more.

We have to be willing to let go of who we are in order to become like Him. Whatever preconceived notions we had about who we are, or what the world tells us we should be, have to be tossed out so He can find room in us to reside.

Bestselling author, C.S. Lewis wrote, "The more we let God take us over, the more truly ourselves we become – because He made us. He invented us....It is when I turn to Christ, when I give up myself to His personality, that I first begin to have a real personality of my own."

Let Him have His way in you so you can truly grow up into the fullness of who He is.

God, who began a good work within you, will continue his work until it is finally finished on the day when Christ returns. (Philippians 1:6 NLT).

8.1 Meditation

References: John 6:63; Matthew 4:4; Psalm 119:9; Philippians 1:6

1. What stood out for you in this lesson?

2. In your own words explain what it means to grow into the Fullness of Christ.

3. Name one person in scripture who was a good example of living for Christ. Why did you choose that person?

4. Do you believe we can grow into the fullness of who Christ is? Explain.

9   Resistance to Change

H ave you ever been at a place in a friendship, job, or group, where you knew that it was time for you to leave, or move on, but you didn't? We often come to these crossroads where life calls upon us to make a decision, but more often than not, we hesitate out of uncertainty and ask ourselves, am I making the right decision? Or, is it the right time to do what I want to do? It could be any number of reasons, but eventually, the hesitation or uncertainty will lead to you feeling stuck if it's not resolved.

I found myself in this dilemma a few years ago. I was a part of an organization where I no longer saw any value in what I was doing. It was next to impossible to do what we were mandated to do because of the prevailing mindsets. No one was satisfied with the status quo yet when change was introduced, they fought it tooth and nails and none could provide a more feasible alternative.

Six years in and we were still having the same conversations as when I started and I had had enough. The bottom line is that I had outgrown that place but hesitated in making the decision to leave because I kept on hoping the situation would change. Even though other people saw, knew and articulated very well what needed to be improved, when the time came to make the change, the majority forcefully resisted. Some were even hostile.

Being an agent of change is not always easy. When I look at the life of Jesus, I see that He also encountered some stubborn people when he was here on earth. The religious people of his time fought against Him and the change He brought. They were more comfortable living in their religious ways than accepting the message of the Kingdom.

The religious spirit always resists change. It is more interested in following outdated man-made rules. It talks a lot about what needs to change but lacks the will to make the change. If not dealt with the religious spirit can hinder a genuine move of God in our lives. This spirit is not only at work in the church, it is also in our personal lives and in our workplaces, as you can see from the example above.

I sat with the Holy Spirit and asked Him to help me examine myself truthfully as to why I wanted to leave, and to also assess the situation rightly. I wanted to be sure that my motivations for wanting to leave were right. In other words, I was afraid of making the wrong decision.

I didn't know where God was taking me. It could be somewhere where I would have to deal with difficult or stubborn people and that environment was good training ground for it. Every moment in that environment provided an opportunity to grow in grace, so I didn't want to leave prematurely.

Jesus did not stop teaching the Message of the Kingdom just because the Pharisees and Sadducees resisted him. He continued to preach and teach and demonstrate the Kingdom of God in the face of it all. So despite the pushback, I continued with what I had to do.

My experience in that place gave me an appreciation for what Jesus experienced when He taught His Kingdom message. The resistance he experienced from the religious factions of His time led to his persecution, arrest and death.

Change can be frightening and many people feel threatened when the things they are familiar with suddenly start to change. Not many people know how to handle change rightly, so they allow fear to hold them back. We resist change because we are afraid of the unknown, but change, although it can be painful, is necessary for our growth. Only when we face that fear can we embrace change and move into our destiny. You are courageous when you face your fears and overcome them.

Nelson Mandela said, "I learned that courage was not the absence of fear, but the triumph over it. The brave man is not he who does not feel afraid, but he who conquers that fear."

After Moses died there was a change of leadership and Joshua became the leader. I can imagine he may have been feeling overwhelmed at this awesome task he inherited from his mentor. Having been with Moses from the time they left Egypt until the time Moses died, Joshua had firsthand experience of the challenges involved in leading the Israelites. To allay any fears Joshua had, the Lord encouraged him with these words:

This is my command – be strong and courageous! Do not be afraid or discouraged. For the Lord your God is with you wherever you go. (Joshua 1:9 NLT).

At least four times God told Joshua to be strong and courageous. This verse of scripture became pivotal for me in my decision making process. I eventually got the release to leave that place and since leaving, God has done such an amazing work in my life that led me to write this book.

Sometimes the thing we are afraid of doing, is the very thing we need to do to see the changes that we want to see in our lives. If you feel that God is leading you to make some changes in your life but you are afraid to do it, I encourage you to push through the fear.

Joyce Meyer said, "Do it afraid." Push through (resist) the fear and embrace faith. Courage is waiting for you on the other side. If you really want to progress and grow in life you cannot be static. You must move forward courageously toward that for which you were called. (Philippians 3:14).

Be strong and courageous.

9.1 Meditation

References: Joshua 1:9; 2 Timothy 1:7

1. What stood out for you in this lesson?

2. Why do people fear change?

3. List two scriptures that talks about dealing with fear of change.

4. How do you handle change?

5. List one other scripture that helps us in our decision making process.

6. How did Jesus handle the people's resistance?

7. What does it mean to be courageous?

10 Who Do You Obey?

T here are some interesting verses of scripture in the book of Luke chapter twelve that I struggled with for a long time. These words were spoken by Jesus, and considering who we know Him to be, the words seemed out of place for my then unrenewed mind.

It took a while for me to get the revelation of what He meant when He spoke those words to the multitudes over two thousand years ago. He said:

"I have come to set the world on fire, and I wish it were already burning! Do you think I have come to bring peace to the earth? No, I have come to divide people against each other! From now on families will be split apart, three in favour of me and two against-or two in favour and three against". (Luke 12:49, 51-52 NLT).

The first time I read it I felt confused. When the angels appeared to the shepherds the night Jesus was born, did they not say, "Peace on earth, goodwill to men"? So how is Jesus saying he didn't come to bring peace on earth?

Sometimes God allows us to have an experience in order to understand what He is talking about. I will use this analogy to explain. Do you notice how your unsaved friends and family all seemed to like you when you were doing what they were doing? You used to see eye to eye with them on many things and even held similar views on cultural topics.

However when you gave your life to God and really began to devote yourself to living for Him, their attitudes toward you changed. Right? That's what Jesus is talking about.

Jesus' message is not a feel good message that maintains the status quo. It demands and inspires change. When that change begins to manifest in your life, even those who were close to you will no longer understand you, and that will sometimes lead to conflict.

When we start to get rid of sinful behaviours out of our lives, it puts us in direct opposition to the world that is still in darkness (ignorance), because they do not obey God's word. In your obedience to God, you have become strange, peculiar to them.

When you are living for God people will misunderstand you, especially if they cannot get you to compromise. I have had people become upset with me and stop speaking to me because I spoke the Word of God in their presence.

The Lord speaks to me in dreams very often. This doesn't make me special, because He does the same with many other believers. The devil will also infiltrate our dreams. I had a dream a little while ago where I saw someone warning or threatening me to stop praying. The individual called me by name in the dream and said, "Be careful of those prayers that you are praying into the earth. Be careful."

I didn't reply. I simply turned around and walked away. How symbolic! Just keep walking. Despite what anyone says or does, just keep on walking in obedience to God.

I laughed when I woke up out of that dream. Obviously my prayers were having an impact in the spiritual realm, so satan saw it necessary to send one of his agents to threaten me. Hahaha.

I couldn't help but wonder where or what is that individual's heart toward me that the devil could use that image/spirit to threaten me. Nevertheless I prayed for the person, asked God to change their hearts and to show them mercy.

In the book of Jeremiah when God first told him that he was anointed to be a prophet, Jeremiah protested. He felt insecure and inadequate to do what God wanted Him to do. Don't we all feel that way sometimes? Sometimes God gives me a word to speak and I second guess whether it was God or my mind. I sometimes convince myself that it wasn't God and as a result, end up disobeying Him.

It is good that He is a God who gives us lots and lots of chances. Nowadays I don't hold back as much as I used to. By faith I do and say what He instructed me to. Why do we hold back when God gives us instructions? Fear. We are afraid that we may be wrong, or it will not be well received and we may end up looking like idiots.

A good way to get over that fear is to look at the prophets in the Old Testament. God gave some of them some really ridiculous (by our standards) things to do and they did it. Isaiah preached naked, Ezekiel was told to bake a cake with human dung, but he petitioned God not to let Him eat anything unclean. So God relented and told him to bake his bread with cow dung instead.

The Lord told Hosea to marry a prostitute and he did. Later when she left him and went back to prostitution, the Lord told him to go back for her and bring her back to his home. By any standards these are hard instructions to follow, yet each of them did as God told them to do.

God responded to Jeremiah's insecurity by saying, "...*you must go wherever I send you and say whatever I tell you. And do not be afraid of the people, for I will be with you and will protect you. I, the Lord, have spoken.*" (Jeremiah 1:7b-8 NLT).

When God told King Saul to destroy the Amalekites in first Samuel chapter fifteen, he was supposed to wipe out the entire nation, leaving nothing. Saul disobeyed God and spared Agag, from whom Haman is descended.

Haman wanted to destroy the Jews in the book of Esther. Had Saul obeyed God, there wouldn't be a Haman. We never know what the end result of our disobedience will be. Saul also kept the best of the cattle and anything that appealed to him.

When Samuel found out what Saul had done, Samuel asked him:

What is more pleasing to the Lord: your burnt offerings and sacrifices or your obedience to His voice? Listen! Obedience is better than sacrifice and submission than offering the fat of rams. (1 Samuel 15:22 NLT).

God rejected Saul as King because he disobeyed His command, and King David was anointed as Israel's next King. God desires our obedience above all, so let us be careful to continue walking in obedience to Him no matter what it costs. He rewards obedience.

10.1 Meditation

References: Luke 12: 49-52; Jeremiah 1:7-8; 1 Samuel 15:22; Hosea 1; Ezekiel 4; Isaiah 20:2-3

1. What stood out for you in this lesson?

2. What did Jesus say He came to earth to do?

3. What can be a source of conflict among family and friends?

4. Which prophets obeyed God, and how?

5. How did King Saul disobey God, and what was the result of his disobedience?

6. Obedience is better than_____.

7. What does this mean to you?

11 It Costs to Obey God

T here is no freedom without sacrifice.

One day after reading the story of Abraham's life those words came to me. Looking back through scriptures we see numerous examples of people who sacrificed to gain freedom, or to step into their destinies - God's calling on their lives.

1. Rahab sacrificed friends and some family members to be rescued from Jericho before it was demolished by the Israelite army. Not much is known about her outside of these events but suffice it to say, she ended up being the great-great-great-(many greats)-grandmother of Jesus.

    She sacrificed to save her household but that sacrifice eventually led to the Ultimate Sacrifice later in the New Testament. (Joshua 2 and 6).

2. Esther sacrificed herself to free the Jews from tyranny and Haman's planned annihilation of her people. Esther knew that she could be killed if she went to the King unsummoned. Yet she put her life on the line for her people. As a result of her sacrifice God caused a turnaround in her situation. Esther's life was spared by the King. The Jews lives were spared and Haman was hanged on the gallows he reserved for Mordecai, Esther's cousin (the book of Esther).

3. Abraham sacrificed much when he left his home and family and everything that he was familiar with behind, in obedience to God's

call on his life. I hadn't really thought about it before now how he must have felt leaving everything he held dear to him behind. (Genesis 12).

I can imagine his family's incredulity at his announcement.

"I am leaving to go to another place. The God who created the universe spoke to me and told me to get up and take my wife and go to a land that he will show me."

I can hear them asking, "The God of the Universe? We don't know this God! How can you follow a God that you don't know? What about our gods? They have been good to us for hundreds of years, now you want to go after a God that you don't know. What? Are you better than us? What makes you so special that this God would talk to you and not us?"

I can just imagine it. Can't you? Whenever God tells you to do something and you are about to step out in faith, you will encounter opposition and negative attitudes meant to deter you from acting on what God told you to do.

This may have happened to Abraham too, even though the scriptures never tell us, but going by human nature I can make that assumption. Their reasoning and taunting may have caused him to go back and check with God to see if He heard him right. On God's confirmation, he told Sarai to "pack up, we're getting out of here." Maybe Sarai had her doubts too but obediently put them aside to follow her husband.

4. The Virgin Mary did not know what she was in for when she accepted the commission to carry the Christ child. By faith she obediently sacrificed her body for this move of God. Imagine what she must have gone through in her community! A pregnant, unmarried virgin. (Matthew 1, Luke 1).

Can you imagine other young women of her time and her age how they might have treated her? She may have been shunned, despised and been called unkind names. Imagine the interrogation from her parents and fiancé? Nevertheless Mary chose to obey God and give birth to Jesus.

When Adam and Eve sinned, humanity lost their connection with God and sin began to rule their lives. The way the world thinks is in direct opposition to God. Therefore for me to give ear to any instruction outside and apart from what God said in His word, or any specific instruction that He gave me, is to:

- Disobey God
- Obey man and in so doing lift him or her up above God
- Be in bondage to someone else's mindset

To walk in the freedom that God has called us to, and to fulfill our destinies requires letting go of some things and people along the way. This is a normal and healthy part of growth although some people would like you to think otherwise.

These are the ones who are trying to keep you where they can control you. They are not growing or doing anything with their lives and want you to remain in that place of stagnation with them. They can become a hindrance to what God wants to do in your life. They will accuse you of selling out, acting like you are better than them, or not walking in love.

As long as you know that you are doing what God instructed you to do and your heart is clean and right with God, take your authority over those lies and shut them down. Pray for those who are coming against you and bless them, and boldly continue to do what God told you to do.

Be careful of Lot – those hitchhikers who wants to ride your train to your destination; a destination that they were not called to. Lot is there to hinder, distract and slow down. (Genesis 13 – 14).

After a time we saw Abraham and Lot parting ways amicably. There will always be separation before elevation. Allow God's natural pruning to happen and don't interrupt it. It was only after Lot left that God took Abraham aside and gave him the vision for his life. After the distraction was removed, God could get through to Abraham.

Hebrews 12:1 NLT, exhorts us to "strip off every weight that slows us down..." Therefore we have to sacrifice them - let them go - and keep moving.

Are you willing to sacrifice to obey God's call on your life?

People are not the only things you will have to let go of. In her Empowering Everyday Women series, Dianna Hobbs says, "The process God uses to get us to our place of destiny often includes leaving some relationships behind, disconnecting from certain associations, relinquishing old roles, taking on new ones, and occupying a strange place."

Old ways of thinking and doing things, which includes cultural and family influences also have to go. Walking in purpose and fulfilling your God-given destiny requires a renewal of the mind, rewiring of the brain or learning to think differently. Forget about what your family or culture says or does and take on Heaven's culture – God's way of thinking and doing things. Let go of those old mindsets and attitudes and allow God to direct your life.

Obeying God is a sacrifice. Sacrifice is painful and gut wrenching but God is faithful to fulfill His promises to you. He rewards obedience.

God is not a man that He should lie; He doesn't change his mind like humans do. Has he ever promised without doing what he said? (Numbers 23:19 TLB).

Are you willing to pay the price?

11.1 Meditation

References: Genesis 12 – 14; Joshua 2, 6; Esther 1 – 10; Matthew 1; Luke 1; Number 23:19; Hebrews 12:1

1. What stood out for you in this lesson?

2. Name two people who made great sacrifices to obey God.

3. What is the spiritual significance of Lot in our spiritual lives?

4. What would you do if someone tells you to do something different from what God told you to do?

5. What does it mean to strip off the heavy weights that easily beset you (Heb. 12:1)?

6. List some things that you must do in order to fulfill your destiny.

12 Pregnant with Purpose

Imagine standing in your backyard on a lovely summer day and poof! Out of nowhere an angel appears. What would you do? I would probably have a heart attack and wet myself at the awesome sight standing in front of me.

Don't laugh. Come over to Luke twenty four with me and I'll show you what I mean. Look at verses four and five. The *Amplified Bible* says:

And while they were perplexed and wondering what to do about this, behold, two men in dazzling raiment suddenly stood beside them. And as [the women] were frightened and were bowing down their faces to the ground, the men said to them, why do you look for the living among [those who are] dead?

See what I mean? If you are still not convinced take a look at Luke chapter one. Zacharias was afraid when he saw the angel and in chapter two the shepherds were terribly frightened when the angels showed up to announce Jesus' birth.

This lesson is not necessarily about angels, it's about purpose, but I had to lay the foundation and prove my previous point.

Purpose speaks of the reason for which a thing exists or was made. Every person on earth came into the earth equipped to fulfill a purpose. You may already know what your purpose is and is walking in it. If you don't, pray and ask the Lord to reveal it to you.

Mary was going about her chores one day when an angel showed up and called her into purpose. Gabriel told her that she was favoured by God. We all know the story of how Gabriel told her that God would use her to do the single most important thing in history; give birth to the Christ child. Exciting! Or is it?

Every God-given calling faces adversity to test its authenticity, and without a doubt Mary faced some adversity as well. We get a little glimpse of it in Matthew 1:19 where Joseph considered putting her away privately. Was it only Joseph who wanted to turn away from her because she was pregnant and unmarried?

The tongues of the young and old women in her community must have been wagging something fierce. Perhaps they even wanted to stone her for allegedly committing fornication. Yet Mary remained faithful to her Godly assignment in the face of it all.

What can we learn from the Virgin Mary?

She was a woman of unquestionable faith. She took the angel at his word and said "be it unto me" without hesitation. She never stopped to ask her parents' permission, nor find out what her fiancé or friends thought of the request. She accepted her assignment without fear or question.

When she went to visit Elizabeth, she went to fellowship with a like-minded person – someone with a similar assignment who was heading in the same direction.

Here was Elizabeth pregnant in her old age. I guarantee that while many may have been happy for her, there were some village gossips who may have felt otherwise. Who then would be more qualified than Elizabeth to understand the highs and lows of Mary's pregnancy? Who else could relate but someone who was experiencing the same thing?

When you become pregnant with a God-given vision, find another (spiritually) pregnant man or woman to fellowship with. Someone who can see what you are seeing, speak what you are speaking and understand where you are in your gestation.

It is important to have someone of maturity, not necessarily in age, but in the spirit. A person of wisdom and discernment who can recognize what you are carrying without you even opening your mouth - whose spirit will bear witness with your spirit.

The scripture said when Mary entered Elizabeth's house all Mary did was greet her. Elizabeth's response was prophetic. She said, *"Blessed above all other women are you! And blessed is the fruit of your womb!"* (Luke 1:42 AMP). How did Elizabeth know Mary was pregnant? By the Spirit.

Surround yourself with godly men and women who will help you carry that vision and give birth to it. Nowadays everything is dependent on networking – knowing the right people who can help you bring your vision to life. Carefully and prayerfully choose who to share your vision with. Be directed by the Lord in this.

Above all, remember that God is your source. He will not allow some people to help you because He alone should get the credit for your success.

In the Old Testament after Abraham and Lot parted ways, Lot was captured by an evil King. When Abraham heard the news, he took 318 of his trained servants and went after Kedorlaomer. He rescued Lot from Kedorlaomer and took back all that they had stolen from Lot. The King of Sodom bargained with Abraham to return the people and keep the goods but Abraham refused.

"I solemnly swear to the Lord, God Most High, Creator of Heaven and Earth, that I will not take so much as a single thread or sandal thong from what belongs to you. Otherwise you might say, I am the one who made Abraham rich." (Genesis 14:22-23 NLT). God alone is your promoter. (Psalm 75:6 NLT).

In one of her teachings Dr. Cindy Trimm reminds us that, "A simple fact of life is that we become like those with whom we closely associate, good and bad. Find people who have the capacity for where you are going, not where you came from."

Paul reminds us in first Corinthians fifteen and verse thirty-three that evil communications corrupts good manners.

A little while ago I was in a place where I was surrounded by a lot of unsaved people. Believers were few and far between in this place and because of the assignment, I had to associate with the unbelievers.

I seemed very strange to them, not participating in their activities, and for the one thing that I chose to do, I always had to spend time in God's presence afterwards to cleanse my spirit of all the filth they were spewing.

That experience made Paul's and Cindy's words real to me. Without the Holy Spirit I would have easily become caught up in all that mess. Satan will put people like these around you to distract and sidetrack you.

When you are carrying purpose you have to have a one track mind. Stay focused. Not everyone can be in your space and not everyone can speak into your life, so be careful who you listen to. "Wise is the person who fortifies his life with the right friendships." (Colin Powell).

Mary was wise in finding a mature, like-minded woman to walk with her. I envision this conversation between Mary and Elizabeth:

Mary:　　　　Elizabeth, I don't mean to be rude, but you are an older, pregnant woman. What are people saying? How do you handle it?
I am young and unmarried. You are married. I hear the things they say about me. It hurts but I keep quiet and talk to God. After all, this thing in me was done by Him. How do I take care of myself in all this?

Elizabeth:　　Don't worry, child. If God gave it to you, He will sustain you. You don't have to take care of yourself. That's His job! Those that know God are happy for me. Then there are the others — them I leave to God. You just nurture what He has given you and listen to Him. This is His will. He will direct us — tell us what to do. Isn't this exciting? God favoring us like this?

- What are you pregnant with?
- What are you going through?
- Have you found your Elizabeth?
- Is she pregnant with the catalyst to what you are pregnant with?
- Does her spirit bear witness with your spirit and vice-versa?

Think on these things.

12.1 Meditation

References: Luke 1, 2, 24; 1 Corinthians 15:33

1. What stood out for you in this lesson?

2. What is the definition of purpose?

3. Do you know what your life's purpose is, or your calling, is?

4. Do you have like-minded people to help you carry the vision? List them.

5. In your own words explain 1 Corinthians 15:33.

6. Who should you share your God-given visions with?

13 Dancing to the Right Tune

I used to have guitar practice every Wednesday. For several weeks my instructor taught me the different scales so that I could solo comfortably over songs. Strumming was easy for me, but soloing was a challenge.

It challenged me to the point where I would get nervous whenever he asked me to solo over a song he was strumming. It was a very intimidating exercise for me because I felt like I couldn't effectively play the notes as I was hearing them in my mind. Due to this I panicked and hesitated whenever he asked me to solo. The fact that I had been doing arpeggios and different finger exercises did nothing to allay the fears.

One particular Wednesday I kept on fumbling my chords. My playing was not sounding good that day at all. I became frustrated but somehow managed to maintain a positive attitude. Later that evening when I was driving home, I began to feel despondent about the session, but something wonderful happened to change that.

I began to think…think properly, that is.

- I had been working with my instructor for a little less than a year at that point, yet within that timeframe I had learned to skillfully play over a dozen songs from memory.
- I had written lyrics and applied music to my own original songs.
- I have played in public twice.
- My skill and confidence in playing had improved significantly during that time.

So why was I feeling down about fumbling over some chords?

Isn't it just like us to drive ourselves to depression by focusing on negative things? We tend to focus on one or two negative things and forget the ten or twenty positive ones.

The sad thing about this is, it wasn't even a negative situation. The fact is I was learning to do something new which required time and concentrated effort. With time I know I would be soloing like a pro, but at that juncture, I was experiencing the growing pains.

I had to get my thoughts in order and remember that I had more going for me than against me. How are you thinking about your situation?

I love to watch Star Trek. I like most of the series in the Franchise but Star Trek: The Next Generation is by far my favourite. Recently I was re-watching the seasons on Netflix and let me tell you, I watched them like I was seeing them for the first time. I was not disappointed.

The episodes were just as good as when I first saw them years ago. In one of the episodes Dr. Crusher, the ship's Doctor, was trapped in an alternate universe. She said, "My thoughts created this universe!"

After going through a series of events where the crew was disappearing from the ship one by one, she realized that she got caught in this "world" because of what she was thinking at the time of an accident in Engineering, during her son's experiment. She now had to think her way out of her dilemma and back into the "real world".

Thoughts are living things. Your thoughts affect your spirit and also the people around you. The scripture says a man is what he thinks. (Proverbs 23:7). Your thoughts also determine how you experience the world around you. Dr. Crusher said, "My thoughts created this universe."

What experiences are you creating in your world? Are you living the life that you desire to live? Are your experiences positive or negative? The answer to each of these is determined by how you think about them. Your thoughts direct your life and shapes your destiny.

Stop right now and think about what you are thinking about. Were your thoughts in line with Philippians 4:8? Be careful what you focus your thoughts on. Thoughts are seeds and the scripture says a bad tree cannot bear good fruit and a good tree cannot bear bad fruit. (Matthew 7:18).

What manifests or fails to manifest in our lives is directly related to our thoughts, so pay attention to the seeds you are planting. Your life will go in the direction of your thoughts.

Who knows what would have happened had I continued to accommodate those negative thoughts. Thankfully I got a hold of myself, corrected that thinking and received the blessings from it. With the help of the Holy Spirit I was able to turn it around and start dancing to the right tune.

13.1 Meditation

References: Proverbs 23:7; Philippians 4:8; Matthew 7:18

1. What stood out for you in this lesson?

2. Why is it important to think good thoughts?

3. What role do our thoughts play in our lives?

4. The scripture says a man is what he thinks. Based on your thoughts, who are you?

5. What are the things that we should think about? List the scripture.

14 Assured Victory

When I realized that God was calling me on my own faith journey with Him, I started studying the life of Abraham closely. In Genesis chapter twenty Abraham and Sarah pretended that they were brother and sister while they were in Gerar.

Abimelech took Sarah and added her to his harem because she was so beautiful. The Lord later appeared to Abimelech in a dream and told him to return Sarah to her husband. He did and also gave them land, silver, sheep, oxen and servants to appease them for what he did.

This puzzled me and I told the Holy Spirit that I would not leave this chapter until He gives me a revelation of it. How does Abraham get rewarded for lying and deceiving the King? If I were to use this as an example, how could I apply it and make it relevant to a current situation?

I got my answer while I was cleaning the house that day. I was reminiscing about how difficult it had been working at a particular job. There was so much resistance from the staff due to the old mindsets that I was coming up against. It reminds me of how most people with religious mindsets treat the Kingdom message of Christ. As Christ said, "You cannot pour new wine into old wineskins."

I remembered the challenges and roadblocks I experienced while trying to introduce a new product. In the end many came to see its benefits, and most importantly, the value of introducing it the way I suggested. Later, the product was described later by an Executive as "the most beautiful thing he had ever seen." Sadly, I felt no joy at hearing this bit of news.

As I thought about it in that moment, I thanked the Lord for being a vindicator and giving me victory. "Lord, thank you for giving me victory in this. I may not have handled all the events as I should have spiritually, but you still vindicated me. Thank you Lord."

Moments later the Holy Spirit spoke to me and said, "That's what I did for Abraham."

When the meaning sunk in I felt joy and laughed out loud. Here is the relevance to something tangible that I was looking for with Abraham's story. I smiled at the wisdom and goodness of God for answering my question.

In every situation, we are given resounding victory in Christ. Even the mistakes work for us when we remain submitted to Him. He knows how to turn it around for our good and His glory. (Romans 8:28).

Thanks be to God, who gives us the victory [making us conquerors] through our Lord Jesus Christ. (1 Corinthians 15:57 AMP).

Meditation

References: *Genesis 20; Romans 8:28; Mark 2:22; 1 Corinthians 15:57*

1. *What stood out for you in this lesson?*

2. *Why did Abimelech give land, silver and cattle to Abraham?*

3. *What mistake did Abraham make in Genesis chapter 20?*

4. *Can you relate Abraham's situation to one in your life? Explain.*

15 The Concealer

A s I was getting dressed for work and putting on my makeup one morning, it made me think about how God takes away our sins and casts them into the sea of forgetfulness, never to be remembered again. (Micah 7:19, Hebrews 8:12 NLT).

I was applying concealer to my face with a blotting motion and I was reminded that He blots out all our transgressions. Applying the concealer effectively blotted out the spots on my face. It concealed (hid, covered) them from outside view.

This is the way the Lord treats our sins when we confess them to Him. He covers, hides, and completely erases them.

I, yes, I alone am He who blots away your sins for my own sake and will never think of them again. (Isaiah 43:25 TLB).

I've blotted out your sins; they are gone like morning mist at noon! Oh, return to me, for I have paid the price to set you free. (Isaiah 44:22 TLB).

In Psalm thirty-two, King David rejoiced in the knowledge that the Lord had covered his sins. He said,

"Blessed is he whose transgression is forgiven, whose sin is covered. Blessed is the man unto whom the Lord imputeth not iniquity, and in whose spirit there is no guile." (Psalm 32:1-2 KJV)

These verses reference sins, transgressions and iniquities as all different things. Are there degrees of sin? No. All sin is rebellion against God. So what is King David saying here?

Let us look at each of these individually:

I.   Sin is the act of rebelling against God, and missing the purpose for our lives if we refuse to repent. When we choose to surrender to the power of evil rather than good, we sin. Sins can be committed intentionally or unintentionally and if we sin, we miss the mark.
II. A transgression is willfully overstepping God's law. When we knowingly commit a sin we are transgressing. For example, when we willfully tell a lie or steal and so on, we are transgressing.
III. Iniquity is more internal. It deals with the state of the heart. An iniquity is a premeditated sin that a person does, and continues to do without repentance. For example David having sex with Bathsheba then having her husband Uriah killed, is considered an iniquity. David's lust for Bathsheba led to premeditated murder.

No matter the type of sin we may have committed, God stands ready to cover them when we repent. Sometimes as women we judge ourselves, and are harshly judged by others, to think that God could never love or forgive us for the things we have done. That is a lie from the devil.

God is no respecter of persons. He treated us all the same when He gave His one and only Son to die on the cross for our redemption. We are the redeemed of the Lord, His inheritance and the Apple of His eye. He holds us securely and He promised that no one can pluck us out of His hand.

So no matter where you find yourself in your walk with God, be confident of his love for you that covers all sins, iniquities and transgressions.

We wear makeup for different reasons: some to deal with oily skin, others to cover blemishes, and others simply as a part of their beauty regimen. Makeup covers temporarily, because once we wash our faces it all goes away and those things which we covered earlier are once again revealed.

But God covers forever – continually. When God covers, blots out, washes us with His blood, the spots and blemishes are gone forever. We become spotless, flawless and clean. You may ask, if that is the case, why do I need to confess and ask for forgiveness?

When you accept Christ as Lord and savior of your life, His spirit seals your spirit. So your spirit becomes clean and pure and flawless, but your soul, where your mind, will and emotions sit, has to be purified.

The soul has to be cleansed of all the unhealthy toxins (thought processes, cultural influences, wrong attitudes) that it has collected over the years, and be brought in alignment with your (perfected) spirit.

As born again believers, we should be God conscious, not sin conscious. However we should examine ourselves on a daily basis to see if we are missing the mark in any way and quickly repent if we find that we are. God does not hold our sins and mistakes against us. He wants to forgive us and He encourages us to confess them to him.

But if we confess our sins to him, He can be depended on to forgive us and to cleanse us from every wrong. And it is perfectly proper for God to do this for us because Christ died to wash away our sins. (I John 1:9 TLB).

Later on in Psalm 32 we see King David confessing to God:

I acknowledged my sin unto thee, and mine iniquity have I not hid. I said, I will confess my transgressions unto the Lord; and thou forgavest the iniquity of my sin. Selah. (Psalm 32: 5 KJV).

Whatever your situation, know that you have a Heavenly Father who is in love with you. Acknowledge and repent of anything in your life which may cause you to miss the mark with Him, and know with all confidence that He's got you covered.

15.1 Meditation

References: Micah 7:19; Isaiah 43:25, 44:22; Psalm 32; 1 John 1:19; Hebrews 8:12

1. What stood out for you in this lesson?

2. In your own words, compare wearing makeup with God's forgiveness.

3. Explain the difference between sin, iniquity and transgression.

4. What does God do with our sins when we repent?

5. What is the difference between the soul and the spirit?

16 Look Within

One of the hardest lessons I had to learn was that my problems were not always external. When things aren't going right, or conflict arises in our relationships, it's easy to point the finger and lay the blame on someone else.

It's their fault. He or she is like this or did that or said such. If he didn't say what he said, or did what he did we wouldn't be in this situation, or we wouldn't be having this argument. It is very easy to lay blame and to think we are always right, but what is your part in it?

Situations like this hardly ever gets resolved if no one is willing to acknowledge how they may be contributing to the problem. If it's always the other person's fault, then the little ember that should have been easily put out, becomes a raging inferno.

In teaching us how to live peaceably with others Jesus encourages us to be quick to examine ourselves first, before pointing the finger at another.

Have you ever got dust or some other foreign object in your eye? It is painful and causes the eye to water, but more importantly it blurs your vision. You will not be able to see properly until that thing is removed.

"It's easy to see a smudge on your neighbor's face and be oblivious to the ugly sneer on your own. Do you have the nerve to say, 'Let me wash your face for you,' when your own face is distorted by contempt? It's this I-know-better-than-you mentality again, playing a holier-than-thou part instead of just living your own part. Wipe that ugly sneer off your own face

and you might be fit to offer a washcloth to your neighbor." (Luke 6:41-42 (The Message)).

In other translations He calls these types of people hypocrites. Jesus is saying remove the distortion from your own vision then you will be able to see your brother or sister more clearly. Look at yourself first!

Until we stop and begin to take stock of our own attitudes and thought processes we are likely to continue having these types of experiences. We have no control over how another person thinks or behaves, but we can do something about our own attitudes and mindsets.

Initially, facing myself – looking at myself through the mirror of God's word - was harder to do than I thought. I saw some ugly things in myself that I didn't know were there. Let me tell you, it is not a nice feeling realizing that you are not as perfect or mature as you thought you were. It can be downright humiliating, but the humiliation is meant to develop humility in you.

The beauty of it is that you are not alone in this. We all have to do it and the Holy Spirit is there to help you. So no matter how ugly something looks, He knows how to turn it around for your good and His glory, when you surrender it to Him.

Get real in His presence. Acknowledge the faults and the flaws. He already knows that they are there, but He needs you to see them so you can surrender them to Him, and go through His transformation process where He will develop your character.

Too many people avoid doing this deep self-examination. It is much easier to blame people and other external forces for our life situations, attitudes and mistakes. However, until we are willing to face ourselves and do the introspective, meaningful change will never happen in our own lives.

Jacob is a perfect example of this. He was known as a trickster. For years he would not admit to who he was. He would not even call his own name. Until one night he had an encounter that changed his life forever.

We know the story of how he stole his brother's birthright and ran away in fear that Esau may harm him. After being away for some time he decided to go back home. On his way to reconcile with his brother Esau, he sent away everyone who was travelling with him so he could be alone.

While he slept in the night, a man came and wrestled with him all night. This wrestling is also a metaphor for Jacob's inner conflict. He had some internal struggles which he had to deal with. First the man or angel wrestled with him, then Jacob wrestled with the angel.

In the latter he told the angel that he would not let him go until the angel blessed him. Even after the angel knocked his hip out of joint, Jacob refused to let go.

The angel asked, "What is your name?"

He replied, "Jacob."

That was Jacob's defining moment. That was the moment he faced himself and admitted who he was. The name Jacob means trickster or supplanter. When he acknowledged who he was, the angel blessed him and changed his name – his identity.

He was no longer a trickster, he became Israel; a prince with God. One translation says he is 'one who has power with God'. (Genesis 32:22-32).

After his night of wrestling the sun rose. Morning came. A new beginning. Jacob started on his journey a new man, even though he now had a limp. The experience changed him and he would never be the same again.

It is important for us to do a regular introspective to see who we are. Only then can we know what we need to change in order to become who we are supposed to be. You must know where you are in order to get to your desired destination.

Go into God's presence and let Him change you. Fight your way into your new identity. It comes with purpose, but you can only come into it after you face yourself truthfully and are willing to make the necessary changes. Then walk boldly into your new day.

Selah!

16.1 Meditation

References: Luke 6:41-42; Genesis: 32:22-32

1. What stood out for you in this lesson?

2. Explain what it means to look within.

3. What is the purpose of doing regular introspection?

4. If you constantly blame others without looking at yourself, you are a _____.

5. What are two things that we need to examine during introspection?

6. When we go into God's presence what should we do?

7. What do you need to do to see lasting change in your life?

17 The Realm of Faith

We have the spirit without measure, but we each have a measure of faith to use proportionately with our gifts and talents. We don't know the exact measure of our faith but it is sufficient for whatever it is needed for.

For He whom God has sent speaks the Word of God, for God does not give the Spirit by measure. (John 3:34 NKJV).

For I say, through the Grace given to me, to everyone who is among you, not to think of himself more highly than he ought to think, but to think soberly, as God has dealt to each one a measure of faith… (Romans 12:3, 6 NKJV).

Belief activates faith. Faith becomes the vehicle that cuts through the fabric of time, goes into eternity and accesses the limitless or unlimited power of the Eternal. It searches the spirit realm finds what we need and transports it from Eternity for manifestation at the right moment in time.

A few years ago, the Holy Spirit showed me this in a dream. I was believing God for something and was vigorously applying the Word to the situation.

I dreamt that I was sitting on a chair and I began to declare the Word of God. As I declared, I moved from sitting to standing on the chair, then later to standing on the table in front of me. This indicated that I was rising to higher levels of faith as I continued to declare the Word.

I spoke the Word over what I was believing for boldly and authoritatively. The atmosphere around me heated up and I could see the heatwaves rising as I spoke. They looked like how heat would look rising off the surface of a road on a very hot day.

As I maintained my declarations, the atmosphere literally collapsed and began to form around the words that I was speaking. The atmosphere took on the shape of the Words and went up into Heaven. Then I woke up.

If ever I struggle to believe for something, I always default back to this dream and it gets me thinking rightly again. Our declarations are powerful. The words we speak have creative power. Like God, we have the ability to create our "world". We determine what manifests in our lives by what we believe and speak.

And God said, "Let there be..." and it was. The Bible says what you decree will be established unto you. Watch your words! Words transcend time and geographical boundaries. They do not expire once released. What you release out of your mouth is at work in the spiritual realm creating what you told it to. What are you speaking over your life, or the life of your children?

Occasionally I do something that I think is very important. I speak into the atmosphere and halt every negative, destiny cancelling, purpose aborting word that I, or anyone else, may have spoken over my life. By faith I pull them down out of the atmosphere, and cancel and nullify them with the blood of Jesus, and render them ineffective in my life. Then I institute counter measures.

I speak the Word of God over my life, my purpose and my destiny, and ask God to help me to speak only His word over me and my future every day. Living in the realm of faith requires us to say what God said at all times, if we are to see the results that we seek.

Now to Him who is able to do exceedingly abundantly above all that we ask or think, according to the power that works in us. (Ephesians 3:20 NKJV).

In the Amplified Bible that same verse is written as: *...abundantly, exceedingly above (more than, surpassing) what we can ask (in prayer) or think (using our imagination to dream) according to the power that works in us.*

That power is the force of faith working by love, in the Holy Spirit. Jesus gave us all of His power before He left the earth, therefore we have all of who God is in us. Nothing should be hard or impossible for us because of that power that is in us.

It is our responsibility to keep the spirit active and working by stirring Him up every day. (2 Timothy 1:6 NLT). If the Spirit becomes dormant, your faith becomes dormant. Faith in God works only by the Spirit.

If Christ's spirit is dormant or dead in us, we would be tapping into another spirit, a faulty power source, which will produce the wrong results. Keeping Christ's spirit active is paramount in seeing the correct manifestation of our faith.

Belief is the key that activates our faith. Faith is the vehicle that drives or flies into eternity, opens the door that fits the particular key that you are using, takes and transports "the goods" back to us in time. This vehicle is fueled by the unlimited power source of the Holy Spirit bringing into manifestation the Yeah of our Heavenly Father, to which we say Amen. (2 Corinthians 1:20 NLT).

The more we use our faith the more it grows. The more we tap into the limitless realm of the Spirit, the more we expand and grow up into it. This is where we ought to live daily. This is the realm of faith; the supernatural.

If I can accomplish it easily then what would God have to do? It's when things seem impossible, when dreams seem unattainable that I need Him to step in. It's when my natural becomes inadequate that I need His "super" to make the impossible possible.

Activate your faith and move into the realm of the supernatural permanently.

17.1 Meditation

Reference: John 3:34; Romans 12:3, 6; Ephesians 3:20; 2 Timothy 1:6; 2 Corinthians 1:20

1. What stood out for you in this lesson?

2. What is the Realm of Faith? How do you access it?

3. How do you activate your faith?

4. How do you keep your spirit active?

5. How do you demonstrate your faith when you are believing for something?

6. The more you use your faith, the more _____
   _____.

7. Name three people in scripture who had great faith.

18 Let It Go

Pain that is not healed will always lead to more pain. You may have heard the phrase, *hurting people, hurt people.* It is therefore important to find and treat the cause of your pain. When we get a cut or bruise, we treat the symptoms of the pain so that healing can occur.

Likewise our emotions and psyche have to be treated with the same care and attention. Unhealed hurt in our emotions can lead to bitterness, anger and resentment, the source of which is unforgiveness. Therefore the quickest way to heal emotional hurts is through forgiveness. Cut the person loose; stop carrying them around and burdening your spirit with all that baggage.

The lovely people of the island of Jamaica use an idiom for when a person is harboring unforgiveness against another. They say, "Him (or she) a carry belly fe me." Translation: He or she is carrying me around in their belly.

Our spirit-man is considered to reside in our bellies, so we can see just how true a statement that is. *To carry belly* for someone is to have an offense against them in your spirit.

You must repent and ask God to forgive you for harboring unforgiveness against that person. You have to release them from whatever the infraction was and ask God to cleanse your spirit of the unforgiveness.

Life is full of tests, trials and afflictions that can rock your world and threaten to destabilize you. These things can either make you or break you; the outcome is entirely dependent on you. Harboring negativity makes

KARLENE MILLWOOD

you bitter. Forgiving and trusting God to help you rise above the situation makes you better.

Stop and ask yourself the question, why is this happening? Is it because of sin in my life? King David says in Psalm 119:67 NIV, *before I was afflicted I went astray, but now I obey your word.*

Is it possible that God has allowed this difficulty in your life to get you back on track? Let's face it. If some of us don't experience difficulties we would never seek God. How much time do we spend with Him when things are going well?

In verse 71 David says, *"It was good for me to be afflicted so that I might learn your decrees."* So is this affliction steering you back on track?

Perhaps you have been in right standing and you are facing a storm. People are coming up against you or your world is shifting. You have been rejected, lied on, abused, lost a job, or lost someone close to you. It is a time to press into God and seek His direction. He may be using this situation to redirect you and take you to another level. No matter what the situation, keep your heart clean.

"If you forgive those who sin against you, your heavenly Father will forgive you. But if you refuse to forgive others, your Father will not forgive your sins." (Matthew 6:14-15 NLT).

Let it go.

18.1 Meditation

References: Psalm 119:67, 71; Matthew 6:14-15

1. What stood out for you in this lesson?

2. Why is it important to forgive?

3. Why does God allow adversity?

4. Is there anyone you need to forgive?

19 Sing, O Barren Woman

I spent some time meditating on Isaiah 54:1 and its relevance to my own life. In this verse Isaiah was encouraging the nation of Israel to burst forth into joyful praise because they would come out of their exile and bear children again.

Earlier in chapter fifty the prophet mentioned that, even though there was a temporary separation, God is not divorced from Israel, and when they return, Israel would once again bear children – more than in their earlier days. My meditation was purely from a woman's perspective though, because I also see this as an encouragement to women who had never given birth in the natural.

"Sing, O childless woman, you who have never given birth! Break into loud and joyful song, O Jerusalem, you who have never been in labor. For the desolate woman now has more children than the woman who lives with her husband," says the Lord. (Isaiah 54:1 NLT).

I have no children of my own – that came from my loins – yet. I am not barren by any means, but the fact that I have not yet experienced pregnancy or childbirth makes this scripture relevant to me, and I'm sure, many of you. I think about the number of children that my life has touched and I see myself in this verse.

There are many children whose lives I have impacted in one way or another. Several of them are now adults with their own children, which makes me a grandmother. Four of these children are my God-children who are near and dear to my heart. I am amazed, and at times humbled, at children's reactions to me when I interact with them. My relationship with them shows a deep level of trust and a mutual affection. It brings home the importance of showing them the same respect that we are asking of them.

Children will remember how we treat them for the rest of their lives. If we treat them well, they will remember. If we treat them bad, they will also remember. How do you want to be remembered? Will you be remembered for bringing direction, joy and laughter to their lives, or will you be remembered for causing hurt and pain?

Let's be clear, I am not insinuating you not discipline a child when it is needed. It is scriptural to discipline them and train them up in the way they should go. (Proverbs 13:24, 22:6; Ephesians 6:4). The question really is, what are you investing into the future generations? What kind of return will your investment yield? Jesus loved children and welcomed them in His presence. I use Him as my example in this. (Matthew 19:14).

You may be single and waiting to get married and have your own children. Or, you are married and believing for God to open your womb and allow you to conceive, or if you have lost a child, be encouraged. Remember that not everyone in scripture got married and had children, and God was still able to use them mightily. You may be a part of this elite group of individuals. Whichever group you fall into, know that God's plan for you is perfect.

He only allows what is purposeful to happen in your life. This may be an opportunity for you to grow in faith. Sarah was ninety years old when she had Isaac. Is there anything too hard for God?

God waited until it was impossible, by human standards, for Abraham and Sarah to have children. They were well past their child bearing years, and had given up hope of ever doing so. Abraham (Abram at the time) asked God, *"What good are your blessings when I don't even have a son? …A servant in my household will inherit my wealth."* (Genesis 15:2 NLT).

God reassured Abraham that he would indeed have a son to be his heir. The promise seemed long in manifesting and Sarah thought she would help God. She encouraged her husband to sleep with her handmaiden, Hagar, who became pregnant and gave birth to Ishmael.

When we move ahead of God, we move out of His will and must be prepared for the consequences. Ishmael was not the promised son and even though he received a blessing as Abraham's offspring, God's will could not be done through him. Fifteen years after God told Abraham he would have a son Isaac was born.

Hannah was a woman who was well accustomed to this plight. For years she couldn't get pregnant, and her husband's second wife, Peninah would laugh at her constantly. (1 Samuel 1). Hannah didn't fuss or fight with her, she took her petition to the Lord. The Lord heard her prayer and she became pregnant with Samuel, who grew up to be a powerful prophet in Israel.

So be encouraged. The same God who moved in Abraham and Hannah's situations is still in the miracle working business. He is the same today as He was in their day. He does not change like shifting shadows. (James 1:17). He takes pleasure in showing Himself off in what seems like impossible situations.

While you wait I encourage you to embrace the little blessings that God may have placed around you. It is mutually rewarding when you give of yourself to a child. No matter how much this world progresses, I still think it takes a community to raise a child.

I thank God for these little blessings in my life. I have more children than I could ever give birth to, yet I still look forward to having my own in God's appointed season. And if it doesn't happen, I am still fulfilled. In the meantime, this woman is singing. Joyfully!

19.1 Meditation

References: Isaiah 50, 54:1; Matthew 19:14, Ephesians 6:4; Proverbs 13:24, 22:6

1. What stood out for you in this lesson?

2. What are your thoughts on Isaiah 54:1?

3. Do you have children of your own? _____

   _____.

4. How could you use this scripture and meditation for yourself or someone else?

5. Pray for those who are:

   a. Still waiting on their season

   b. Have difficulty getting pregnant

   c. Have lost a child

20 A Special Gift

C hildren are special to me. I love their natural exuberance about life. I love the sound of their laughter and how their little eyes twinkle like they have a galaxy of stars in them. I love the purity of a child's heart. If a child loves and trusts you, you will know. If they don't, you will also know.

I also love the cautiousness of children. I love how they take their time in getting to know a person before entrusting themselves to that person. Their little spirits are being discerning. This is an important practice that many adults have forgotten.

Children are God's gifts to humanity. They are the continuation of ourselves, therefore we each have a responsibility to bring them up in a healthy way. It is important to create healthy environments for them, ensure proper nutrition, clothing, shelter; all the basic necessities of life.

When a child is raised in a healthy environment it shows. The Bible says, *"Train up a child in the way he should go, so that when he is old he will not depart from it."* (Proverbs 22:6 KJV).

A part of that training is how to interact with others. These are skills that are learned in the immediate family. If the family environment fosters positive attitudes, positive self-image, respect for others and their property and privacy, it will show.

Discipline plays an important role in child rearing. *Those who spare the rod of discipline hate their children.* (Proverbs 13:24).

Some in our modern society do not discipline their children as they ought, while others take discipline to the extreme. As with all other things, discipline has to be handled with wisdom and in moderation. There is a fine line between discipline and abuse. This is the part I have issues with. We all should have issues with it.

Abuse is ugly and can kill physically, emotionally and spiritually. A child who has suffered abuse can carry the scars throughout their lifetime. If not healed, these scars can color their lives one way or another. I absolutely hate the thought of a child being abused. It angers me.

God pays attention to how we treat our children – these precious gifts that he has entrusted to us. He hates abuse. It is a diabolic spirit from the pit of hell. *Jesus says, "Whoever welcomes one of these little ones in my name, welcomes me. And whoever welcomes me does not welcome me but the one who sent me."* (Mark 9:37 NIV).

In this one scripture God shows us how intimately and intricately He links Himself to children. It stands to reason then that:

Whoever abuses one of these little ones, abuses Me. And whoever abuses Me abuses the Father.

Whoever hates one of these little ones, hates Me.

Whoever hurts one of these little ones, hurts Me.

Whoever loves one of these little ones, loves Me.

Whoever cares for one of these little ones, cares for Me.

Get it?

In Matthew 18:10 NIV He says, *"See that you do not despise one of these little ones. For I tell you that their angels in Heaven always see the face of my Father in heaven."*

Abuse is evil and God hates and abhors all evil. He has established certain judgements for evildoers and as He says in the book of Revelations, He is coming with His reward in His hands to pay every man according to their work. (Revelation 22:12). Therefore there are eternal consequences attached to how we treat our children.

Think about this with your own children, and the children you will encounter throughout your lifetime. Be a part of the solution and let us take care of the little ones and bring them up in the fear and admonition of the Lord.

If you, or someone you know, is or have been abusive in the past, you can turn it around. Repent of it. Denounce it and ask God to forgive you. Get in His presence and let Him reveal the root of it and ask Him to heal you. Talk to your pastor or another person you trust who can help you.

If you are a survivor of abuse and may still struggle with the memories, forgive. Forgive your abuser or abusers. Forgive those who despitefully used you and abused you, then do as the scripture says and call yourself blessed. (Matthew 5:11).

This does not have to define you or determine your future. God is still a healer and he knows your end from the beginning. He loves you. Nothing that you, or I, have done or experienced can stop our Heavenly Father from loving us. (Romans 8:35, 38).

You are also His special gift.

20.1 Meditation

References: Proverbs 13:24, 22:6; Matthew 5:11, 18:10; Mark 9:37; Romans 8:35, 38

1. What stood out for you in this lesson?

2. How important are children in our world? Why?

3. What is our responsibility to the children in our lives?

4. What role does discipline play in a child's life?

5. What role does abuse play in a child's life?

6. How would you handle an abusive person?

7. What should you do if you think you are an abusive person?

21 Show A Child Some Love

I believe that May is the best month of the year. Let's face it, May is just reflective of the sunny disposition of the ones that claim it as their birth month. Right? I say yes because it is the month of my birth.

Coincidentally May is the month that I look forward to receiving applications from the little ones for the scholarship I created to help with their education. I excitedly anticipate the receipt of these essay applications yearly. It gives me insight into the children's dreams and aspirations, and the challenges that they are facing academically or otherwise. I read through them with love, paying attention to the little details that make me connect with them on a personal level.

Looking after the little ones and investing in their future is one of my passions. Just writing that sentence put a big, old smile on my face. When we care for, protect and nurture them we also care for, protect and nurture a purpose. Every child comes into this earth with a unique purpose, therefore it is important to create the right environment for them to grow to their full potential.

Unfortunately this is not always the case in our world. News reports are rife with stories of sex trafficking, pedophilia and other types of abuse of our young ones. Militant groups like ISIS and Boko Haram are well known for their exploitation of children. ISIS is training boys as young as ten to be jihadists, while Boko Haram, which means Western education is a sin, is enslaving mostly female youngsters. It is based on their flawed ideology that women should not get an education, but should be home taking care of husbands and children.

I believe the age-old saying that "it takes a community to raise a child" still stands in the twenty-first century. Let us care for our little ones, whether we are their parents or not. One way to do this is by becoming a mentor. One of the most rewarding things that I have done so far in my life was to partner with the Big Brother, Big Sister Foundation as a mentor. There are many children who need mentors in their lives and should you decide to take on the challenge, I guarantee that it will be mutually beneficial for you and the child or children.

As believers, we have much that we can teach them, and fulfill the mandate to raise our children in the fear and admonition of the Lord (Ephesians 6:4). Psalm 127:3 NLT says, *Children are a gift from the Lord; they are a reward from him.*

Parents, I encourage you to spend quality time with your children, teaching and admonishing them in the ways of the Lord. Leave work at work, turn off the TV, get rid of the distractions and give yourself to your children. They need you more than they need things.

So while you are buying the latest gadgets or clothes for them, remember they need you more. I agree with Luis Pasteur when he said, "When I approach a child, he [or she] inspires in me two sentiments; tenderness for what he is, and respect for what he may become." For the rest of us who are not (yet) parents, become a mentor and invest in a young life. Show a child some love today.

21.1 Meditation

Reference: Ephesians 6:4; Psalm 127:3

1. What stood for you in this lesson?

2. What does the Bible say about raising children? Provide scriptures.

3. When we invest in the life of a child, what are we really doing?

4. How can we invest in children?

22 True Passion

A few years ago, after watching Mel Gibson's Passion of the Christ for the first time, I asked the Lord to do something for me. The movie had touched something deep within me and I found myself sobbing openly, and at times, uncontrollably. No matter how many times I have watched the movie since, it elicits the same response.

Pictures speak volumes. Personally, I grasp a lot more out of a picture than a paragraph of words. I can read words over and over and still not grasp their meaning, but seeing something visually brings an almost immediate understanding. Many times I imagine or visualize something that I am reading. Getting those images involved also helps make the meaning clearer to me. The imagination is a powerful tool given to us by our Heavenly Father and plays an integral role when we are exercising faith.

The Passion of the Christ brought to life words that I read on a page for many years, only partially understanding the sentiments behind them. This movie made the suffering of Christ real to me. I was drawn into each scene and became caught up in the moments, yelling at those who were insulting Jesus, then laughing at myself afterwards for doing so.

Something happened as I watched Jesus' response, or lack of, to these insults. Words began to take on new meaning through pictures and an emotional cocktail of pity, anger, grief and sorrow acted as a detox. I convulsed, my shoulders shook, I clutched my stomach and fell to my knees and wept bitterly.

For about two to five minutes I stayed in that position wallowing in grief at the realization of what Christ endured for me. For us. I spontaneously fell prostrate on the floor and cried out, "Lord, teach me to love like you." Over and over again, I whimpered these words to Him. When we pray we want God to answer but when the answer comes, we are unprepared for it.

God's answers don't always manifest in the way we expect them to. I would have liked to wake up one day and have the supernatural ability to love like Jesus. Of course that is not how the answer came. The answer came in a series of tests similar to what Jesus endured. I was insulted, disrespected, falsely accused, betrayed, rejected, cursed, humiliated, lied about and ostracized. Things were happening so quickly, and all at the same time. It was intense.

I did not know how to handle it, because I was not relating it to the prayer that I had prayed. I could not see the similarities in my situation to Jesus' persecution. I was looking with natural eyes and not spiritual eyes. Suffice it to say I responded in the natural. I failed this process numerous times. With every failure the devil would beat me up with defeating thoughts. I felt unworthy and demoralized.

Feelings of despair and condemnation overtook me and it seemed like I would never be able to get out from under them. I felt like a failure, and when chastisement came, so did the feelings of shame and condemnation. As these emotions took hold, it was more than I could bear and I spiraled deeper into an abyss of defeat and rebellion.

The more I felt defeated, is the more I rebelled. The more I rebelled is the more I was chastised. This cycle went on for a long time before I came to my senses. The devil had setup so many strongholds in my mind and was trying to convince me that there was no hope for me. He was telling me that I was damaged goods and that I would never be healed, or delivered from these things. I became depressed and I isolated myself from those who truly cared for me.

Only when I began to understand who I am in Christ, did any of this change. The more I understood my sonship in Christ, the more I understood and accepted His love, the more I opened myself to receive His forgiveness, the more I believed what the Word of God said about me, then and only then did I come up out of satan's grasp.

I came across the scripture which says, *"So now there is no condemnation for those who belong to Christ Jesus. And because you belong to Him, the power of the life-giving Spirit has freed you from the power of sin that leads to death."* (Romans 8:1-2 NLT).

I realized that Christ, through His passion, had already freed me from the very things that were holding me captive. I just needed to accept it. As I meditated that verse and other scriptures which spoke of His love for me, I was able to rise up from that pit of despair and condemnation.

God is not keen to hold our sins against us. The enemy wants us to think that God is perpetually angry at us if we make mistakes, so we can turn away from our loving Father, but he is a liar from the beginning. Satan wants us to be weak and defeated so he can continue to rule our lives through ignorance – his greatest weapon against the church.

That is why it is important for us to study the word of God and know it for ourselves. The only way to get rid of ignorance is by getting knowledge. It is the Word of God that will help us to win the battle against the devil. It is the only thing that satan cannot withstand. That is why he works so hard to get us to doubt God and His word, or to keep us too busy that we cannot spend time reading the Bible.

The Apostle Paul said in 2 Corinthians 5:19 NLT, *"For God was in Christ, reconciling the world to himself, no longer counting people's sins against them. And he gave us this wonderful message of reconciliation."*

God no longer holds our sins against us. It does not mean that we go out and sin indiscriminately without repenting. We all strive to live according to the Word of God, but at times we may inadvertently miss the mark. When we make honest mistakes, God doesn't hold them against us. Committing premeditated sin without repenting is a whole different ballgame. We must examine ourselves daily to know where we stand in our faith walk.

If you sin in any way, repent quickly. He is a loving God who will forgive you quickly and erase that sin from your record. We are no longer slaves to sin because Christ freed us through his finished work on the cross. We are new creations. The old life has past and we are now living a new life. When we understand the depths of God's love for us, we will never struggle to overcome satan's lies anymore.

Coming into this level of understanding helped me to stand up to the tests when they came my way again. When I was faced with those spirits of deception, lies, rejection and so on, I was able to overcome them. Even though they caused pain, I was able to release it to the Lord, forgive those who were coming against me, and love them anyway.

Through it all my prayer was answered, and I am learning to love like Christ more and more every day.

22.1 Meditation

References: Romans 8:1-2; 2 Corinthians 5:19

1. What stood out for you in this lesson?

2. Explain what it means to love like Christ.

3. How should you deal with feelings of condemnation?

4. What scripture or scriptures talk about this? Explain.

5. What did Christ's death accomplish? List scriptures.

6. What can you say about God's love for us?

23 What Has God Said?

W hat has God said?

Stop focusing on how it looks and focus on what God said. *God is a King and where the word of the King is, there is power and authority.* (Ecclesiastes 8:4 AMP).

What has God said?

Remember that whatever a King says (decrees) becomes law. Once it becomes law it cannot be reversed, not even by the King. The King's will always stand. The King's word is His will.

What has God said?

- I am blessed. (Matthew 5; Genesis 12:3).
- I am a son of God and the righteousness of God. (John 1:12; 2 Corinthians 5:21).
- Wealth and riches are in my house. (Psalm 112:3).
- I am the head and not the tail. (Deuteronomy 28:13).
- I am a lender and not a borrower. (Deuteronomy 28:13).
- Whatever I touch will prosper. (Deuteronomy 30:9; Psalm 1:3).
- No weapon formed against me shall prosper. (Isaiah 54:17).
- By His stripes I am healed. (Isaiah 53:5).
- I am called, anointed and appointed. (Jeremiah 1:5).

What is God saying about your situation?

- I will make a way in the wilderness and rivers in the desert. (Isaiah 43:19).
- I open doors that no one can shut, and shut doors that no one can open. (Isaiah 22:22; Revelation 3:7).
- You will laugh at your enemies. (Psalm 37:13, 59:8).
- Do not fear! (Isaiah 41:10).
- Be strong and courageous. (Joshua 1:6-9).
- I can do abundantly exceeding more…(Ephesians 3:20).
- Your future is fixed and no one can stop it. (Romans 8:29; Job 42:1).
- You are secure in me. (John 10:28-30).
- I watch over your going out and coming in. (Psalm 121:7-8).

For we walk by faith, not by sight (2 Cor. 5:7).

Believe! And say what God said.

23.1 Meditation

References: Genesis 12:3; Deuteronomy 28:13, 30:9; Joshua 1:6-9; Ecclesiastes 8:4; Esther 8:8; Job 42:1; Psalm 1:3, 37:13, 59:8, 112:3, 121:7-8; Isaiah22:22, 41:10, 43:19, 53:5, 54:17; Jeremiah 1:5; Matthew 5; John 1:12, 10:28-30; Romans 8:29; 2 Cor. 5:7, 21; Ephesians 3:20; Revelation 3:7

1. What stood out for you in this lesson?

2. The contents of this lesson are mostly _____.

3. Why are declarations important?

4. The Word of the King has _____.

5. What is a decree?

6. What is it called when we speak the word of God over ourselves?

7. We do not walk by _____. We walk by _____.

8. How do you activate your faith?

24 Dealing with Conflict

I don't know about you, but I don't like conflict nor dealing with conflict. I dare say this is residual from the old way of thinking, and yes I am working to change it. For if we understand the purpose of conflict, we wouldn't abhor it or run away from it when it comes our way.

Conflict arises to help us grow. Without conflict we live the status quo and run the risk of becoming comfortable and stagnant. Stagnation makes you irrelevant and obsolete. Conflict comes to shake things up and force us to think differently, become better problem solvers and rise to another level.

So be truly glad. There is wonderful joy ahead, even though you must endure many trials for a little while. These trials will show that your faith is genuine. It is being tested as fire tests and purifies gold. So when your faith remains strong through many trials, it will bring you much praise and glory and honour on the day when Jesus Christ is revealed to the whole world. (1 Peter 1:6-7 NLT).

I love to watch Star Trek. My favourite series in the Star Trek Franchise is The Next Generation. In one of the episodes the Enterprise and its crew were catapulted into an area of space that no other vessel had ever visited, by immature 'deity' and their archrival, Q.

They encountered a vicious alien race called The Borg, and had to find their way back to normal space before The Borg started assimilating them.

When they returned to normal space, they knew it wouldn't be long before The Borg tracked them there, but the encounter prepared them well to face that enemy when they showed up. At the end of it all, Captain Picard summed it up like this, "Perhaps what we needed was a kick in our complacency to prepare us for what lies ahead."

When things are going well in our lives we tend to become complacent. God is not interested in our comfort, He is interested in our growth. Myles Munroe puts it this way:

"When we become complacent, God will allow adversity to test and prepare us for the next level."

Do you notice that when conflict or adversity comes, it comes from different angles? It never is just one thing, but a series of things to deal with at the same time. Someone once told me, "God gives His biggest test, to His mightiest warriors."

Are you a mighty warrior looking for a big reward? Then rest assured that your test will be a big one. Before David went to fight Goliath, He asked, *"What will a man get for killing this Philistine and ending his defiance of Israel?"* (1 Samuel 17:26 NLT).

David felt he was well able to defeat Goliath. He had killed a lion and a bear with his bare hands on the backside of the mountain while tending to his sheep, so this guy was nothing for him to handle.

The King promised one of his daughters as a wife to Goliath's killer and tax exemption for the man's entire family. (1 Samuel 17:24-27). David accepted the challenge to battle Goliath and received his reward.

It is impossible to go through life without dealing with conflict, so you might as well change your mindset about it, and learn how to deal with it effectively.

Most conflicts arise from misunderstandings – sometimes petty ones. When two dissimilar viewpoints are expressed about a particular issue it can lead to conflict.

Sometimes the conflict is from those closest to you. When God is drawing you into purpose, you will feel an overwhelming urge to spend a lot of alone time with Him. During this time, many will misunderstand what God is doing in your life, and may take it the wrong way.

Even though your separation from them is not personal, they may still misinterpret it to be so. Misunderstandings like these often lead to conflicts in our relationships. Talking things out doesn't always guarantee an amicable ending. You have to be confident that you have done your best in the situation, then release it to God.

When you are walking with God, there are certain places on the journey where it will only be you and Him. After Apostle Paul had his encounter with Jesus on the road to Damascus, he went away to Arabia for three years to be alone with the Lord.

Sometimes you have to get away from the crowd. Get by yourself and get quiet in His presence so He can download His instructions to you, heal you and minister to you. If not, you could miss important information and delay God's purpose manifesting in your life.

Having gone down Delay Avenue before, I am intent on being in the will of God as He leads me down Destiny Highway. You must do the same.

The devil will setup obstacles and distractions to derail you, but you remind him that no weapon that is formed against you will prosper. Every obstacle that presents itself is an opportunity for you to rise higher. You have to dig in your heels and be determined to do what God told you to do, and go where he told you to go.

Keep vigilant in prayer no matter what is being said or done during these times. Hold your peace and speak only when God tells you to, and only to whom He leads you to speak to.

Many will become angry when you begin to walk on your predestined path. The attacks will come when you are not doing what people want, or expect you to do, because they can no longer control you. You will not be well-liked when you begin to become the true version of yourself. Don't let that stop you.

They may ridicule you or withhold their support when you choose to obey God and move into His calling on your life. Rest assured that God has your best interests at heart. He is teaching you to depend on Him alone.

He allows certain things to happen so you can grow in wisdom, and know who or what to avoid. You will begin to discern those around you more clearly, and be able to avoid the trap of being held in bondage by any toxic thinking.

When Moses went to deliver the Israelites out of Egypt, Pharaoh held him at bay for a long time. God had to send a number of plagues on Egypt before Pharaoh relented and let the people go. This was a conflict to end all conflicts.

While they were on their way they came to the Red Sea. They could see no way around this obstacle. To make matters worse when they looked behind them, there was Pharaoh and his army pursuing them to recapture and take them back into captivity. They panicked.

But Moses told them, "Don't be afraid. Just stand still and watch the Lord rescue you today. The Egyptians you see today will never be seen again. The Lord himself will fight for you. Just stay calm." (Exodus 14:13-14 NLT).

That's a word for you. Just stay calm. Do not fear or become panicked. When the devil raises his ugly head and starts to snarl at you, just stay calm. Stay in the presence of the Lord and keep on listening to Him. He will give you instructions on what to do.

How would the Israelites get out of this dilemma? Moses listened to the Lord. Throughout the entire ordeal, Moses spent a lot of time talking to, and listening to God for instruction.

So here they are at the Red Sea. The Lord told him to take his staff and stretch it out over the water and divide the water. He did as the Lord told him and the Israelites were able to cross over on dry ground, and the enemy that was chasing them were all drowned when the waters came back together.

God removed the obstacles out of their way and delivered them out of the hands of the enemy. God has never lost a battle and He knows how to make a way out of no way. He will always show you the way out.

Remember that people are human and are prone to making mistakes. Be willing to please God more than people. Despite how much you love them, be careful to obey God and let His will manifest in your life.

Your families and friends mean well, but many of them may not have the capacity for where you are going. Find those who have the capacity for where you are going and run with them. Love your family and friends. Pray for them and bless them, but know that you may have to leave them behind in order to fulfill God's purpose and calling in your life.

Remember that you cannot control how another person thinks or behaves. You can only control your own behavior and attitude. Submit yourself to the Lord, and trust Him in all things.

24.1 Meditation

References: 1 Samuel 17:24-27; Exodus 14; 1 Peter 1:6-7

1. What stood out for you in this lesson?

2. What are some things that cause conflict?

3. What is the best way to handle conflict?

4. What is the purpose of conflict?

5. What are some things to pay attention to during a conflict?

6. How can you overcome adversity caused by conflict?

25 Do You Really Trust Him?

Every so often I ask myself this question, then stop and think to be sure I am being truthful when I answer, yes. There was a point in my life when nothing seemed to be working. I was doing all the right things, staying in faith and trusting God, but still nothing seemed to be working. To make matters worse, it seemed that I was caught in a perfect storm of family conflict, business issues and relational tension.

I was being hit from three different angles. Negative situations were coming from everywhere and it seemed never ending. I was in prayer night and day about this because some of it started to get into my spirit. I constantly spoke the Word of God over myself and over my life to counter the negativity, and also prayed earnestly for those coming against me.

To add to it all, I was in the middle of planning an event and everything seemed to be going as planned until the day of the event when we were surprised by a freak snow storm. Attendance to the event was minimal to say the least, but turned out to be the best in quality of all the events I had done before. Irony of ironies!

God was faithful and caused a turnaround the day after the event when the gospel jazz artiste that I brought in from out of town, was able to minister at my local church. The anointing flowed through him into that saxophone and hit the congregation with powerful precision. Many were on their knees or prostrate worshipping God as a result. To God be the glory.

During the same time period a young man showed up in my life. He made all the right moves to the point where others took notice and, for lack of a better word, became excited at the prospect of a love interest for me.

Truthfully I was more cautious. At a certain point in our interaction the Holy Spirit impressed on me strongly certain questions that I should ask him. I asked and got the answers and when I did I understood that the Holy Spirit truly is a protector.

Dealing with all this at the same time felt overwhelming, but in those moments I remembered the scripture which says, *God causes all things to work together for good for those who love Him and are called according to His purpose.* (Romans 8:28 NASB). I realize that no matter what I was facing, God was in full control.

Nothing happens unless He allows it, and if He allows it then there is a purpose for it. What was the purpose of all of this? I did not get the answer right away but over time I came to see the blessing in each of these situations. The bible says, *So when your faith remains strong through many trials, it will bring you much praise and glory and honor on the day when Jesus Christ is revealed to the whole world.* (1 Peter 1: 7b NLT).

As for the young man, we parted ways amicably, but I got a greater sense of confidence and comfort in knowing that the Holy Spirit will always lead me to make the right decisions. When the time comes for me to say "yes" to someone, the Holy Spirit will be right there with me. In this I am confident.

I realized how much I grew as a result of each of these situations. I was stronger mentally and emotionally and my faith level had increased. By the looks of it nothing was going my way, but spiritually things were unfolding as they ought.

Trust Him in all things.

25.1 Meditation

References: Romans 8:28; 1 Peter 1:7

1. What stood out for you in this lesson?

2. What does it mean to trust God?

3. Is God aware of everything that happens to you? Explain.

4. What should you do when things aren't going as you expect them to?

5. Do you trust God? Give an example.

26 Knowledge is Key

I gnorance will always attack what it doesn't understand. This thought came to me while I was cooking one day. I thought about how we sometimes wrongly assess situations. It reminded me about what our pastor taught from Hosea 4:6a (NIV). It says, *My people are destroyed for lack of knowledge. Because you have rejected knowledge, I (God) also reject you as my priests.*

This was written to Israel but also applies to so many facets of life today, in and outside of Christ. Those outside of Christ are operating according to world standards which is in opposition to God's laws. Many of us are saved but we still live our lives ignorant of who we are, of our identity in Christ, and of our position in Him as sons of God.

In either case, when we don't understand what God, who is love, requires of us, we will continue to treat each other contemptuously; despising each other for things of a trivial nature. We will cut each other down with our words and cause hurt and pain with our actions. The only remedy for this is love.

When we operate in love, we operate from the person of God, for God is love. However until we are taught God's way we cannot come into this nor see it manifest in our world. God knows this and has put a plan in place. It is revealed in Jeremiah 3:15 (AMP). *I will give you shepherds after my own heart who will lead you (or teach you) knowledge and understanding [of God and His ways].*

Let's face it. Ignorance is a lack of knowledge, isn't it? So how best to conquer ignorance than to get knowledge? King Solomon tells us in

Proverbs 4:7 KJV, *"wisdom is the principal thing; therefore get wisdom. And in all thy getting, get understanding.* Wisdom is born when understanding meets knowledge. Get knowledge. *Study to show thyself approved unto God, a workman that needeth not to be ashamed, rightly dividing the word of truth.* (2 Timothy 2:15 KJV).

Someone once said, "The greatest enemy of the church is not the devil, it's ignorance." Satan is able to rule our lives only through ignorance. So the more we increase in Godly knowledge, the less room satan has to work. In addition to the Bible, read books that will educate and enlighten you. Use every opportunity to drive out the darkness of ignorance by turning on the light of knowledge. Only fools hate knowledge. Don't be a fool!

For the Lord gives wisdom; from his mouth come knowledge and understanding. (Proverbs 2:6 ESV).

26.1 Meditation

References: Hosea 4:6; Jeremiah 3:15; Proverbs 2:6, 4:7

1. What stood out in this lesson for you?

2. How important is it to get knowledge? Explain.

3. What is the difference between knowledge, wisdom and understanding?

4. List some scriptures outside of the book of proverbs that speaks of them.

5. What does the Bible say about people who reject knowledge?

27 A Father's Love

I was singing the popular worship song, Thou Art Worthy, taken from Revelation 4:11 one night. *Thou art worthy, O Lord, to receive glory and honor and power: For thou hast created all things, and for thy pleasure they are and were created.*

As I sang, it was impressed in my spirit that I am saying 'I love you' to God the Father. The impression on the inside is that God created man to rule the earth, but before He created man He created every resource man would need. So when we think of Him as Creator, and God the Father who gives us all things including Himself, we can do nothing else but say Thou art worthy or I love you.

It's like a child who received a most precious gift from a good father that he or she is close to. The child may lovingly cling to the father's leg or hug him around the neck and say, "Daddy, I love you!" The act of endearment was prompted by the Father's benevolence. Likewise our adoration of the Heavenly Father is prompted by who He is as Father. A good father.

I thought of my step-father who loves me dearly. The feeling is very mutual. He came into my life when I was four years old and has been there ever since. Even though his relationship with my mother ended many years ago, his relationship with me has continued over the years. Neither one of us letting go of the other.

Despite the differences between him and my mother, he never stopped loving me or thinking of me as his daughter. Coincidentally, as I write this summary, a gospel jazz song by Kirk Whalum is playing in the background with the words, "don't ask me how or wonder why I could love you like I do, it's cause you're mine, it's cause you're you. Don't ask me why, it's what I do." How very fitting!

Beautiful words from our Heavenly Father to us. While I reminisce on the love of an earthly father, my Heavenly Father is extolling His love to and for me through this lovely rendition, sung by Lalah Hathaway. The Lord is perfect in all He does. I felt like the Lord was telling me that, just as how the differences between my mother and step-father didn't stop my step-father from loving me as his child, likewise there is nothing or no one who can stop the Heavenly Father from loving me.

"Can anything ever separate us from Christ's love?" The Apostle Paul asked in Romans 8:35 NLT. *"Does it mean He no longer loves us if we have trouble or calamity, or are persecuted, or hungry, or destitute, or in danger, or threatened with death?"* That covers every situation we could find ourselves in.

I am convinced that daddy was sent into my life to show me a father's love that would last a lifetime. There is nothing in this world that could stop my daddy from loving me. Likewise, there is nothing on earth that could stop our Heavenly Father from loving us. Paul confidently assures us, *"And I am convinced that nothing can ever separate us from God's love."* (Romans 8:38a NLT). Enough said.

I am convinced of this truth. Nothing beats a father's love.

27.1 Meditation

References: Revelations 4:11; Romans 8:35

1. What stood out for you in this lesson?

2. How does the Heavenly Father express His love for us?

3. Describe one way God has revealed Himself to you as Father.

4. What does the love of a good father look like to you?

5. What will stop the Heavenly Father from showing His love to us?

28 Effective Communication

H eaven has a mandate to reestablish good upon the earth, but it needs clear communication lines so that it can receive requests for what is needed, as well as hands on the ground to implement the strategies and distribute to the needs! (Cindy Trimm). [1]

We interact with humanity through communication. Communication is not only about conveying words to another. Approximately ninety percent of communication is non-verbal, which means our emotions, body language, tone of voice and frame of mind play a big part in how we deliver and process information. When everyone is thinking on the same wavelength, understanding flows, and it makes communicating easy. However life is not always that way.

It can be problematic when we don't communicate well with each other. Faulty communications can lead to misunderstandings, unwanted tension and create conflict. Good communication is peaceful, fosters feelings of well-being and promotes a sense of oneness among the communicators. Effective communication is the glue that helps us deepen our connections to others, and enables us to convey even difficult messages without creating conflict or destroying trust.[2]

So how can you ensure that you are communicating effectively? One of the things that I do is to repeat what the other person said to me in my own words to ensure that I understood them correctly. That way, if I have misinterpreted what they said to me, they can correct me right there and

---

[1] The Art of War for Spiritual Battle
[2] Helpguide.org

then. Effective communication is paramount if we are to see the results that we want to see in our lives.

A few years ago I was assigned to a project at work. This project had a high profile internally and externally to the organization. The stakes were very high. As a result a very political mood pervaded every aspect of the project, and many of the participants jostled to 'look good' to those in authority, and would use any means to achieve their goal.

When I read the above paragraph in Trimm's book, it made me think of that project and that time in my life. If you know anything about project management, the project manager usually kicks off the project by assessing the needs or requirements of their customers. These are then translated through the other people or technology, to meet the customer's desired goals at the end of the project.

Issues soon arose in producing reports that the customer requested. This was due partially to inaccurate requirements that the customer provided to the project manager, which was passed down to me and then translated by me to the programmers. In addition to that, our team found out that we had done analyses on the wrong set of data which led to more errors in the output.

The root cause of these issues? Communication. Poor communication. Due to misaligned communications many hours were wasted, and the aftermath was messy. People started to blame each other or gloat, depending on which side you were on, about mistakes being made, but still, what should be done was not getting done because everyone was still communicating out of context.

Prayer is our way of communicating with Heaven. We see how important this practice is in Jesus' life as he prayed often to His Heavenly Father. The disciples, seeing his devotion to prayer, and the power that flowed from Him as a result asked him, *"Lord teach us to pray."* (Luke 11:1).

Looking back at Trimm's paragraph, I have to wonder if my prayer life is like what she described, or if it was like the gobbledygook ways of communicating that I experienced on that project. Clear, effective communication is as important in the spiritual as it is in the natural. Even more so. Therefore when we pray our prayers have to be specific if we want to see the right results.

James says, we *have not because we ask not and when we ask, we ask amiss.* (James 4:3 KJV). If it is not focused, clear communications, we will get similar results to what we got on the project I described earlier; a lot of wasted time and faulty results. Then we may become like the participants and blame God for not answering our prayers, instead of looking at where we may have missed the mark, and seek to make the necessary corrections.

James tells us again in chapter five verse sixteen that, *the prayer of a righteous person is powerful and effective.* It is clear, focused, effective communication to God that gets you the results that you need. The Lord desires us to come to Him with boldness and present our requests clearly. *"Present your case," the Lord says. Bring forward your strong arguments,"* the King of Jacob says. (Isaiah 41:21 NASB).

The best way to achieve this is to use God's word back to Him. Find the scripture that relates to your situation, if you don't know it from memory, and read it straight from the Bible. Put Him in remembrance of His word. (Isaiah 43:26). That way you are hitting the target with precision and angels begin to move on your behalf to fulfill your requests.

The word of God is powerful and active. It is meant to get results. In the Amplified Bible God says it like this through Isaiah, *"So shall My word be that goes forth out of My mouth: it shall not return to me void [without producing any effect, useless], but it shall accomplish that which I please and purpose, and it shall prosper in the thing for which I sent it."* (Isaiah 55:11 AMP).

If you want to live a successful, purposeful life full of blessings and good results, ask God to help you communicate clearly to Him and to those around you.

28.1 Meditation

References: James 4:3, 5:16; Isaiah 41:21, 43:6, 55:11

1. What stood out for you in this lesson?

2. What method do we use to communicate with God?

3. In your own words, describe effective communication.

4. Why is accurate communication important?

5. How can you ensure that you are communicating clearly to God?

6. What's the key to living a successful life?

29 Feasting with the King

When Buckingham Palace holds a banquet it is with much glitz and glamour. Men and women don their best in honour of the Queen. The Queen also goes to great lengths in choosing her attire and has a lot of say in the planning of the event. She honors every visiting head of state by wearing the highest honor available of their country. Everyone dines on specially prepared menus and dance to appropriate music. The Queen and visiting head of state always address the guests by giving a speech before they eat.

Picture the splendor of such an event at Buckingham Palace. Now think about the fact that we, as believers in Christ, also belong to a Kingdom. One that is more resplendent than the British Monarchy, headed by an even more benevolent King than the reigning Queen of the United Kingdom.

In all their splendor, no earthly dominion could ever measure up to the Kingdom of Heaven. In Matthew twenty-two Jesus tells a parable of a king who prepared a wedding banquet for his son. None of the invited guests wanted to attend the banquet so the king became angry and advised his servants, *"Now go out to the streets and invite everyone you see."* (Verse 9).

The servants complied and invited everyone that they could find to attend this banquet. The King joined the banquet later and found a man who was not properly dressed for the occasion. He commanded his servants to *"bind his hands and feet and throw him into outer darkness, where there will be weeping and gnashing of teeth."*

Wait a minute. This man and the other guests all received a last minute invitation to this banquet. This means he may not have had the time to go home and change, and not wanting to keep the King waiting wore what he had on to the banquet - to his demise. What harsh punishment! This tells me that we must be prepared at all times to go into the presence of the King. The truth of the matter is that we live in the presence of the King, therefore we must always be clothed in our righteous attire, and be ready to be called upon for His use at any time.

When He makes a visitation we must be ready to commune with Him, and not have to worry about going to change our clothes (repent). The word must be hidden in our hearts so that we are ready to give a word in season and out of season. The Bible tells us of ten virgins who went out to meet the bridegroom. Five of them were prepared and the other five were not. When the bridegroom made his appearance at midnight, only the five who were prepared were allowed to go in. The others missed their opportunity because they weren't ready. (Matthew 25:1-13).

God requires a certain standard from us when we approach Him in worship. Worship is not only about singing songs and making declarations. Our lifestyle should be lived in such a way that whatever we do honors the King. The Psalmist asks these questions, *"Who may climb the mountain of the Lord? Who may stand in His holy place? Only those whose hands and hearts are pure, who do not worship idols and never tell lies. They will receive the Lord's blessing and have a right relationship with God their savior."* (Psalm 24: 3-5 NLT). This is the standard of God's righteousness that He expects us to live by.

Another feast is spoken about in the book of Revelations chapter nineteen, called the wedding feast of the lamb. Verse 7 and 8 in the New Living Translation says, *"Let us be glad and rejoice, and let us give honor to Him. For the time has come for the wedding feast of the Lamb, and his bride has prepared herself. She has been given the finest of pure white linen to wear."* Pure white signifies righteousness or holiness. The Lord desires righteousness from us. *But just as He who called you is holy, so be holy in all you do, for it is written: "Be holy, for I am holy."* (1 Peter 1:15-16 NIV).

Were we to be invited to Buckingham Palace for a feast with the Queen, we would be sure to put on our best before going in her presence. Why wouldn't we want to be attired in our best for a meeting with the King of Kings?

Notice that Queen Elizabeth herself is dressed in her finest before her subjects and visiting heads of state. So is our Lord. His robe is sparkling white for He is the holiest of all. Therefore He requires the same of us when we go into His presence. "Be holy for I am holy." In other words, dress properly, because I am properly dressed.

What is a banquet without food? Most banquets that I have attended ensure that they provide fine, multiple course gourmet meals to the attendants. Only the best of the best is served at a banquet at Buckingham Palace. Yet fine foods alone is not sufficient. When satan tempted Jesus in the wilderness to turn the rocks into bread, Jesus gave him a simple answer. *Jesus answered him, "The Scriptures say, 'It is not just bread that keeps people alive. Their lives depend on what God says.'"* (Deuteronomy 8:3; Matthew 4:4 ERV).

Food can be healthy and unhealthy. Healthy food nourishes the body and helps to minimize the risk of sickness and disease. Unhealthy food does the opposite. The rise in the consciousness of the populace for a healthy lifestyle has seen several health food stores opening up in North America over the past few years. One of the most well-known is Whole Foods.

Whole Foods pride themselves on providing good quality products. They stand out from the crowd because of their position and branding in the marketplace. Their prices are also premium based on the quality of their products. You pay more for quality.

Feasting with the King, is to read and meditate on His word. David said, *"I study your words very carefully so that I will not sin against you."* (Psalm 119:11 ERV).

Just as bad food and unhealthy eating habits can lead to deficiencies and other health issues, so a life without the word of God can suffer from deficiencies. A healthy dose of God's word guarantees healthy living. The Word of God must be taught and ingested in its pure, potent form. Nowadays many people are mixing new age practices and ideologies in with scripture. Wherever the word of God is diluted, you will find a weak and stagnant congregation. Why? The people perish for lack of knowledge.

The Word of God is alive and active. God guarantees that His word is designed to do what He sent it to do, so when we water it down, it loses the effect that it is supposed to have. Weak word, anemic faith. Potent (strong) word, strong faith. It's that simple.

I encourage you to spend time feasting on the Word of God and hear what He is saying to you through the Spirit. When you read, ask Him to rest on you with the spirit of wisdom and understanding, revelation and insight, counsel and might and knowledge and the fear of the Lord. He will enlarge your territory; expand the borders of your mind, and increase your capacity for understanding His word. You will see the Word start to become alive to you. You will begin to see things that you never saw before, and the King and His Kingdom will start to become more real to you.

Spend time feasting with the King. It's a most important prescription for healthy living.

29.1 Meditation

References: Deuteronomy 8:3; Matthew 4:4, 22:9–13, 25:1-13; Psalm 24:3-6, 119:11; 1 Peter 1:15-16

1. What stood out for you in this lesson?

2. What does it mean to feast with the King?

3. What standard of living does God require of us?

4. What produces weak or strong faith?

5. Explain the importance of living by God's Word.

30 A Cup of Coffee

B y the time I saw him, his arms were outstretched and he was practically screaming, "Cup of coffee? Cup of coffee?"

It was a cold morning and he was sitting on the sidewalk in only a pair of light grey pants and a tattered shirt. His feet were bare and his hair unkempt. I, on the other hand, was well covered in my work attire plus a warm coat, scarf and gloves, but I still felt cold. My initial thoughts were for his health. Isn't the ground cold? I hope he won't get sick from sitting down there, I thought.

A lady in dark pants and a grey coat walked right by him as if he weren't there.

"Cup of coffee?" he asked loudly as she went by.

I stood on the opposite side of the street waiting for the light to change. My eyes were riveted on him and I felt a twinge in my belly and wondered if this is what it meant when the scriptures said Jesus' insides were twisted up with compassion when He thought of the plight of Jerusalem. (Luke 19:41-44).

I felt sorry for him. I wondered what had transpired in his life to get him to this stage, and whether he would or could ever find his way back. A faint chirping signaled that the lights had changed and I started walking. His eyes focused on mine and he stretched his hands out towards me. Desperation comingled with frustration when he asked, "Cup of coffee, Miss? Anything you have will help."

I rummaged in my handbag to find my purse. He stood to his feet in anticipation and like an excited child about to get a toy he prompted me, "it's only a buck sixty-five. A toonie (CAN $2.00) would suffice."

"I'm sorry. I don't have any change," I told him.

The light in his eyes dimmed but soon regained their lustre as I continued.

"If you follow me into the coffee shop I will purchase it for you with my debit card. Would that be OK?"

"Oh yes, Miss. That'd be just fine."

He practically skipped behind me into the coffee shop, found a table at the back and sat down.

"May I get you something to eat with the coffee?"

"No, Miss. All's I want is a cup of coffee."

I took the coffee from the attendant and handed it to him. His fingers curled around the cup as if it was a most cherished possession.

"Thank you, Miss. And God bless you. Just a cup of coffee, that's all I want."

I waved goodbye and wished him a good day, then felt like a hypocrite for doing so. I wished I could do more for him.

It doesn't take much to show a little bit of kindness and compassion. Jesus was always taking care of the poor when he was on earth, so much so that when Judas left the last supper to betray Him, the other disciples thought he went to give money to the poor. (John 13:29)

Look for opportunities to do good every day.

30.1 Meditation

References: Luke 19:41-44; John 13:29

1. What stood out for you in this lesson?

2. List at least one scripture where Jesus talks about the poor, and what He said.

3. What does it mean to you to be compassionate?

4. How might Jesus handle this situation if He were still on earth?

31 Facing the Giants

I n order for us to trust God with the big things, we have to first learn to trust Him with the little ones. As we receive the answers to the little things, it builds our faith to believe for bigger things.

God is interested in even the small things in our lives and will give us experiences to prove it to us. One day many years ago, I was getting ready to go to the pharmacy to buy toothpaste and other toiletries. I was heading through the side door into my garage when my front doorbell rang. It was my neighbor.

She handed me a small shopping bag and said, "I hope you use these things. I bought them but I don't need them and thought of you."

I thanked her and shut the door. When I opened the bag, it contained the very items that I was going to buy. What a nice surprise! I hadn't even prayed and asked for them. I thanked God then cancelled my trip to the pharmacy. Similar things have happened for me since that day and with each one, my faith level increased. Now I believe Him for much bigger things, and as those manifest, it expands my capacity to believe and trust God even more.

He has developed me in this area so much that now I trust Him for everything. I consult Him before I do anything or make any decisions. I trust Him to direct me where He wants me to go and to do what He wants me to do. When I have the assurance that He has led me into a place or an activity, then no matter what comes, I am able to face it with the knowledge that He is with me. I have His protection because I am in the centre of His will.

Scripture is filled with people who went down in history and received commendation from God because of their faith. By faith:

- Noah built the ark
- Abraham obeyed God
- Sarah conceived at ninety years old
- Joshua made the sun stand still
- David slayed Goliath
- Jesus did many miracles

By faith I left my home and moved to a new city where I knew no one, for one year, when He told me to. Being in an unfamiliar place was disconcerting at times, but I knew who I was with and who was with me. This book was birthed out of that journey.

David honed his fighting skills on the backside of the mountain tending sheep and writing poems and songs to God. He killed a lion and a bear with his hands alone, so when it came time to confront Goliath, he felt confident that he could take him, and he did.

When David refused to fight in King Saul's armour it didn't mean that he was weak or afraid to rise to the challenge. Look at what David did afterwards. He defeated the enemy that had all of Saul's army cringing in fear for weeks. David simply fought in his own skin (in his authenticity, at his own level), from a position where he was comfortable.

As a shepherd he was skilled at using a slingshot. He hadn't been trained to fight in an army so he was uncomfortable in the armour. They were unfamiliar to him and made him feel clumsy; out of his element. He gave them back to Saul and went outside and picked up five smooth stones and set off to confront the Philistine.

You are not ready to face your giants until you know who you are. You must know who you are and whose you are. Unless you understand and accept your sonship through Christ, the enemy will defeat you. Don't pretend to be who you are not, or where you are not in the spirit. Be authentic. Be real. Acknowledge where you are and let the Holy Spirit develop your spiritual muscles. He alone knows how to get you to where you need to be.

He perfects the things which concerns you and makes the crooked places straight. Rest assured that God will never give up on you. He has invested too much in you to leave you by the wayside. He is interested in your success because His reputation is tied to it. You are the only one who can stop what God wants to do in your life. Mistakes and people cannot stop it. He causes all things to work together for you, so He can turn around even the mistakes. It stops only if you give up. If you stop believing. If you let go of your faith.

God's will for you can only stop if you shrink back, and if you do, *He takes no pleasure in you.* (Hebrews 10:38). *He leads me in the paths of righteousness for His name's sake.* (Psalm 23:3 AMP). His name's sake simply means because His reputation depends on it. Another way to look at it is to bring honour to his name.

David knew who he was and confidently stepped out of Saul's covering and trusted God. *"You come to me using sword, spear and javelin. But I come to you in the name of the Lord All-Powerful."* (1 Samuel 17:45 ERV).

David had all the covering he needed, the Lord Himself, to face this fierce enemy. The scripture says the Name of the Lord is a strong tower. The righteous run into it and they are safe. David was confident of the Lord's power and protection. It was his confidence in the God of his victories that gave him the courage to face Goliath and bring him down.

As New Testament believers we are supposed to wear God's armour daily. Paul encourages us to, *"Put on every piece of God's armour so you will be able to resist the enemy in the time of evil. Then after the battle you will still be standing firm."* (Ephesians 6:13 NLT). It's not something that we wake up and put on every morning, we live in it every moment of our lives, so that we are ready to face and bring down the enemy's strategies every time.

David honored God that day in a way that Saul never did. He put His faith in the abilities of the God he came to know while tending sheep. David's faith moved God and God gave him the victory over Israel's biggest enemy. He later went on to win many battles as King, and persevered through much adversity. Today, not only is David remembered as a man after God's own heart, but also as a victorious King and a fierce and powerful warrior.

David proved God in the little things, and when he was faced with the big nine foot giant, his faith in God was at a level where nothing seemed impossible to him. Don't ever think anything is too small for God to care about in your life. He cares about every detail of it. Prove Him in the small things and let Him build your faith and prepare you to face the giants.

31.1 Meditation

References: 1 Samuel 17; Hebrews 10:38, 11; Psalm 23:3; Ephesians 6:13

1. What stood out for you in this lesson?

2. What does it mean to face the giant?

3. What is the most important thing you need to face your giants? Explain.

4. Explain what it means to be authentic.

5. Why did David give Saul's armour back to him?

6. What is the armour of God, and what does it mean to wear it?

32 The Bully

April 10th has been designated as Pink Day in North America. Although it is now being used to show solidarity with a certain social group, its origin goes back to a school in Nova Scotia, Canada, where a young boy was bullied for wearing a pink shirt to school one day. His friends all decided to wear pink to school afterwards to support him, and pink day was born.

Cyber bullying has become popular in recent years, and is equally as dangerous as the other forms of bullying. In April 2013, a Canadian teenage girl committed suicide as a result of cyber-bullying. She made a bad decision two years earlier to drink vodka at a friend's party where she became inebriated. In her state of drunkenness four boys gang raped her, photographed the incident and posted the pictures on Facebook. The emotional turmoil from the experience was too much for her and she ended up taking her life.

As someone who was bullied for many years as a child, I denounce bullying in any form. It is wicked and harmful to the victim. Unfortunately for me, the child that used to bully me lived near me growing up, so it was next to impossible to avoid her. I remember the fear I felt whenever I had to leave my home to go anywhere. I usually breathed a sigh of relief if I managed to go out and return home without encountering this antagonist. Many days I went home in tears feeling beat up and helpless after a run in with this child, who I will call Tanny.

Until one day I had had enough and decided to fight back. I was returning home from a wedding when I saw Tanny sitting by the side of the street. The moment I laid eyes on her I purposed in my heart, "I am not taking her nonsense today". I calmly approached where she was sitting and walked by without even looking at her. She picked up a rock and threw it at me. It connected. I turned around and my right foot connected with her left cheek.

Stunned, she looked at me like I had lost my mind. I calmly turned and started walking away. Moments later I was shoved in the back and I almost fell forward. I turned around and grabbed her and we became locked in a battle grip. In my heart I had decided that today was the day when I killed her. There was a steep drop on the other side of the road. If she didn't let me go I decided to drag her there and push her over, even if I had to go with her.

We wrestled with each other and with each step I pushed her closer to the edge. Tanny was a strong girl. It was no easy feat maneuvering her to where I wanted her to be. Suddenly I felt a surge of strength and I pushed her hard. We were only a few inches from the edge at this point, when I heard someone shouting, "No! No! Don't do it!"

One of the adult neighbours saw what was happening and figured out my plan. When he shouted, Tanny also caught on to my intention. She pulled my dress over my head to distract me. My underwear was in full view for everyone to see. Under normal circumstances it would be embarrassing, but at that moment I didn't care. I was intent on achieving my goal.

With my dress covering my face it was difficult to see and it broke my momentum enough to allow the neighbor to reach us and pull us apart. He gave us both a stern scolding and sent us on our way.

Suffice it to say from that day Tanny never bothered me again. Nowadays, as adults, when we meet, she treats me with the utmost respect, and I stop and talk with her, holding no grudges. I am glad I had the courage to face the bully that day and change my situation for good.

This story is not meant to condone or promote violence in any way. Nor is it meant to suggest we retaliate and take vengeance on our enemies. The Lord said vengeance belongs to him, He will repay. We are supposed to forgive, bless and pray for our enemies. (Deuteronomy 32:35; Romans 12:19; Matthew 5:44). At the time when this happened, I was a child and that is how I dealt with it. The only way to deal with a bully is to confront him or her. You cannot overcome what you don't confront.

Likewise, we have a bully in our spiritual lives who, much like Tanny, does not relent in his harassment of the saints. Satan is always lurking in the shadows looking for a way to get at us. He stalks us and tries to terrify us by throwing out terrors, arrows, diseases and disasters. He is persistent in his harassment of God's people – he doesn't let up.

That is why Peter encourages us to, *"Stay alert! Watch out for your great enemy, the devil. He prowls around like a roaring lion, looking for someone to devour."* (1 Peter 5:8 NLT).

If we don't know our enemy, or how to deal with him, we will be overcome by his tactics and live a beat up, defeated life. He is not supposed to overcome us, we overcome him because greater is He that is in us, than he that is in the world. (1 John 4:4).

Sun Tzu, a general and strategist in the Chinese military hundreds of years ago, wrote some insightful strategies on how to deal with the enemy in a time of war. His beliefs have had a profound impact on Western culture and have been quoted in many books and at many leadership conferences.

I read some of these insights and three of them had meaning for me. Sun Tzu said:

i. If you know the enemy and know yourself, you need not fear the result of a hundred battles.
ii. If you know yourself but not the enemy, for every victory gained you will also suffer a defeat.
iii. If you know neither the enemy nor yourself, you will succumb in every battle.

The key then is to know yourself and the enemy. Become aware of satan's tactics and his strategies. How does he come at you? What are the things he likes to throw at you? Some of his ways of operating are to:

- Bring up things from your past to try to embarrass you
- Spread gossip and slander to assassinate your character
- Attack your body through sickness and disease

He makes any and every kind of noise to get you distracted but I encourage you to keep your eyes on the Lord. The scripture says, *"When anyone is in Christ, it is a whole new world. The old things are gone; suddenly everything is new."* (2 Corinthians 5:17 ERV).

When you come to Christ and accept Him as your Lord and Saviour, you are set free from whatever you did in the past, or anything that was done to you. You are not defined by your past because Christ has made you brand new, and He who began a good work in you is faithful to complete it. He knows how to use your past for your good and His glory, so satan has nothing on you. That is why you have to know who you are and whose you are.

Tanny pulled up my dress and my underwear was exposed, but notice what I said. In that moment I didn't care. I stayed focused on the task at hand. Hold on to your faith! You have to come to a place where you are so hidden in God, that satan's attempts to embarrass, humiliate or distract you fails. Tanny's objective was to distract me from what I was doing, and hinder me from seeing where I was going. Satan works the same way. No matter what he does stay focused and maintain your position.

When my eyes were covered by my dress, *it broke my momentum.* This is important to note, because this is exactly what satan wants to do to you; to break your momentum. To slow you down. To hinder your progress. Satan will use many ways to create a storm to try to get you in fear and pull you out of faith.

In Mark chapter four after Jesus had finished teaching and was crossing to the other side of the Lake, a fierce storm rose up and the boat began to fill with water. While the disciples were panicking and bailing water, Jesus was sound asleep. When they woke Jesus in the midst of their panic, what did Jesus do? He immediately drew on His faith. He rebuked the wind and the waves and they became silent, then he asked the disciples, *"Why are you afraid? Do you still have no faith?"* (Mark 4:40 ESV).

Bullies operate the spirit of intimidation. It is meant to put the other person in fear. That was satan's intention when he stirred up that storm and he had the disciples where he wanted them. In fear. But Jesus approached it from a positon of faith and the storm had to back off. It's either faith or fear – never both. They cannot work together. Fear connects you with satan, while faith connects you with God. So which will you choose? When you know the enemy's strategies you will know how to defeat Him.

Knowing your position in Christ as a son of God makes you secure and confident. Knowing yourself and knowing your enemy gives you the advantage, and satan's ammunitions can't destabilize you. Knowing who you are, enables you to confront the bully and send him fleeing every time. Study the word of God and get to know Him. Learn who you are in Christ, and learn how the enemy works then apply your faith in every situation.

Be relentless, because the devil is relentlessly stalking you. Be determined to attain that goal of a higher calling to which God called you. Don't allow the enemy to push you back, slow you down, or hinder you from moving forward. Fight the good fight of faith with fortitude. Take your battle stance, confront the bully and stand!

32.1 Meditation

References: 1 Peter 5:8; 2 Corinthians 5:17; Mark 4:40

1. What stood out in this lesson for you?

2. Why can we compare satan to a bully?

3. When someone hurts or harms us, how should we handle it?

4. Who else in scripture can be described as a bully?

5. What are some of the tactics satan uses against us? Provide scriptures.

6. How should we respond in these situations?

33 Addiction

Addiction. It's a word that to one extreme evokes images of rundown, dismal, dingy crack houses with strung out junkies masked by white smoke swirling all around. Or, it could be that a person is an enthusiastic devotee to a particular thing like sweets, gambling, sex, shopping and now, social media. Either way any habit left unchecked can become addictive.

The word addiction carries a negative undertone so it is not usually associated with good images. Is it possible to become addicted to something good? And if you do, is it a bad thing? Hmmm…Research has proven that social media can be as addictive as drugs and alcohol, and is a very real source of stress. Over use of social media has been linked to high levels of credit card debt, low credit score and some instances of overeating.

How do you know if you are addicted to something? Psychologist, Doctor Jill Grimes says, "If the thought of giving up a habit for a week produces anxiety, then you may have a problem."

A week?

A while back some folks and I took a little hiatus away from using Facebook. On its own it is not a big deal, but then there were those who were wondering, and even questioned why we had not been posting much recently. So, as a challenge, we decided to minimize our Facebook usage for a month. If I did not have to check important messages sent to my inbox, I would not have used it at all for that month. And you know what? My world didn't crumble and business didn't stop.

In the grand scheme of things life went on normally and I proved to myself that I can still live, work and play without Facebook. No addictions here. As for the others, they only visited to play games. Or so I'm told (smiley face).

We make dozens of choices in our lives every day, good and bad. Bad choices, if continued over a period of time, creates a pattern that lead to toxic thinking. Believe it or not, we can also become addicted to thoughts, negativity, complaining and other undesirable attitudes and behaviours. In one of her presentations on toxic thinking, Dr. Caroline Leaf says, "When we make a bad choice we throw our mind into neuro-chemical chaos. Bad choices have an impact on how our brain develops and functions. Our choices, which are the consequences of our thinking, can literally turn our genes on or off."

Dr. Leaf is a believer in Christ who is also a Neurosurgeon, and has done extensive study, and ground-breaking research on the mind and the brain and how they function. It is her belief that addictions are a result of bad choices that we make. Bad choices cause negative reactions in our brains. These negative reactions can alter our physiology and lead to sickness and disease. Good choices also have an effect on our brains. They alter our physiology for the good. Therefore bad choices are connected with death and good choices lead to life.

It is important to be aware of what we are thinking and consequently what we are speaking. James tells us the damage that can be caused by an untamed tongue. In the same breath he said no one can control the tongue. Yet it is vitally important to watch what we say. If our brains and physiology can be altered by bad choices, then our speech will also be affected by it. What fills our minds will come out of our mouths, and we steer our lives with our words.

[3] We put bits into the mouths of horses to make them obey us. With these bits we can control their whole body. [4] It is the same with ships. A ship is very big, and it is pushed by strong winds. But a very small rudder controls that big ship.

And the one who controls the rudder decides where the ship will go. It goes where he wants it to go. [5] It is the same with our tongue. It is a small part of the body, but it can boast about doing great things. (James 3:3-5 ERV).

What we think is activated only when we speak. Before God spoke creation into being, He spent time thinking about it. When it was perfected in His thoughts, He spoke it forth. "Let there be..." There was a manifestation for everything He spoke. Where are you steering your life? The scripture says, *"The tongue can speak words that bring life or death. Those who love to talk must be ready to accept what it brings."* (Proverbs 18:21 ERV). Therefore think and speak deliberately.

We reap a harvest based on the seeds we plant. If the seeds (thoughts) are good, we can expect a healthy harvest, and the opposite is also true. Jesus spoke about this in the book of Luke. He said *good people say good things because good things are stored in their hearts. Bad people say bad things because of what is in their hearts. "What people say with their mouths comes from what fills their hearts."* (Luke 6:45 ERV). Heart in this context is referring to the mind.

With the understanding that addiction begins in our thoughts, and that our thoughts influence our speech and our actions, we can conclude that it is also possible to become addicted to something good. Being addicted to the things of the Kingdom of God is always good and only good will come from it.

"Blessed are those who hunger and thirst after righteousness, for they shall be filled." (Matthew 5:6 KJV). We were created to be addicted to our Heavenly Father and His word. This is the only addiction that humanity should have. Abstaining from this for a day, much more a week, is what should make us anxious.

Yet unfortunately so many ignore God and His word and listen to so-called experts who are not more than educated fools. This is a very bold statement but the scripture says the fool says in his heart, there is no God. The Hebrew translation of this is, in his heart, the fool has said 'no' to God.

Many of these experts do not believe in God and want nothing to do with Him. What source are they connected to? Where are they getting the information that they are promulgating? Are they feeding you truth or lies? That is why we should never argue with unbelievers or atheists about the things of God. Why argue with a fool?

King Solomon's advice is, *never answer a fool, or you too will look like a fool.* (Proverbs 26:4 ERV). I love how Mark Twain says it. "Never argue with stupid people, they will drag you down to their level and beat you with experience."

Spending time with God and His word has great benefits for the believer. His word is life and health to us, and the solution to every problem can be found in it. The answer to reverse any negative addictions is right there in the word of God, so use the good to counter the bad.

God's thoughts toward you are good. He wants you to be successful and when you become full of His word, you will speak what's in your heart and direct your life to the hope and bright future that God has destined for you. Are you addicted to social media? How long can you give up using social media before anxiety kicks in? If not social media, what are you addicted to? Are you addicted to the Word of God? Food for thought.

33.1 Meditation

References: Proverbs 18:21, 26:4; Matthew 5:6; Luke 6:45

1. What stood out for you in this lesson?

2. What is the cause of an addiction? Do you agree with this observation? Explain.

3. What are some things people become addicted to?

4. What should we become addicted to? Why?

5. Can an addiction be reversed? How?

6. What can a thought be compared with? Explain.

34 Conforming

I have spent a lot of time thinking about how easy it is to conform.

Conform (v):   To act in accordance with prevailing standards, attitudes, practices etc.
To be or become similar in form, nature or character.

Looking at the definition of the word, conforming in and of itself is not a bad thing. Where it may become problematic is when we think of who or what we are conforming to. Most people are comfortable going with the crowd because to do otherwise would make them stand out, be different, and not everyone is comfortable being *different*.

To go against the grain is to call attention to oneself and not necessarily welcomed attention. Certain standards, attitudes and ideas have permeated our culture and become societal norms over the years and we are expected to fall in line and get with the program. As The Borg from the Star Trek Franchise would say, *Resistance is Futile*. When you choose to be different there may be repercussions -- real or imagined.

But…

There is a guy that I look up to. He's my hero. A non-conformist in his day whose actions turned the known world upside down. Jesus went against the grain of his society when he was on earth in human form and caused a revolution of mass proportions. We are still experiencing the ripple effects in the 21st century.

If I am to conform (become similar in form, nature or character) to anything or anyone's ideals, this is the one I choose to conform to. Yet the irony is that many find *Him irrelevant and His teachings archaic*, to borrow a phrase from the stage script of my friend Michelle Richards-Reyes. His message is one of freedom, true freedom, empowerment, dominion and peace. The very things that most people desire to live a fulfilled life yet they denounce what He represents. How can you find true fulfillment in life when you reject the source of it?

I could go on about this but I will leave you with this thought:

Don't copy the behavior and customs of this world [or conform], but be a new and different person with a fresh newness in all you do and think. Then you will learn from your own experience how his ways will really satisfy you. (Romans 12:2 TLB).

Did I get you thinking? Resistance is NOT futile.

34.1 Meditation

References: Romans 12:2

1. What stood out for you in this lesson?

2. What is the difference between conformation and transformation?

3. How does Jesus' message lead to: (Provide scriptures)

   a. Freedom:

   b. Empowerment:

   c. Dominion:

   d. Peace:

35 Do Not Despair

S o you are at a place in your life where things are flowing smoothly. Things are good at home, at work and in your relationships with family and friends. It seems like you are on a ship cruising the turquoise blue waters of the Caribbean Sea.

The sunshine glistens on the gentle crystalline waves. There you are basking in the beauty of it all when suddenly...wham! Your peace and tranquility are rudely interrupted by an external force and you go careening into a wall. You get some bumps and bruises and experience some pain, but you are still alive, albeit shaken by the sudden impact.

Isn't that the way life is sometimes? Let's face it, things don't always go the way we plan them and things can go awry even with the best laid plans. If you are in that situation today do not despair. As a child of God you have His assurance that He will never leave you nor forsake you. You are well known to your Heavenly Father, therefore nothing about you, or your life surprises Him.

Jeremiah 1:5 reminds us that He knew us before He formed us in our mothers' womb. In Psalm 139:16 we are reminded that every day of our lives was recorded in His book before one of them came into being. In that same chapter we are reminded that there is nowhere that we can go where the Lord's spirit cannot find us.

Adversity comes to teach us important life lessons. Every challenge we face is designed to help us regain the knowledge of who we are and to direct us to a greater purpose for our lives. So no matter how hard things get, or how you feel, push through.

Whatever God allows in our lives have purpose. Therefore adversity is not for our destruction, it is for our growth and development. It is in the hard times where we grow in strength, patience and perseverance. It is in these hard places where we prove who our God is. Adversity provides an opportunity for God to show Himself off in our situations. So do not despair.

In Luke 12:6-7 NLT, Jesus says, *"What is the price of five sparrows—two copper coins[b]? Yet God does not forget a single one of them. [7] And the very hairs on your head are all numbered. So don't be afraid; you are more valuable to God than a whole flock of sparrows."*

Be encouraged today. Your Heavenly Father knows you by name. He knows the number of hairs on your head. You are worth more to him than many sparrows. His thoughts about you are vast and deep, and He will never leave you nor forsake you.

Don't worry about anything; instead, pray about everything. Tell God what you need, and thank him for all he has done. [7] Then you will experience God's peace, which exceeds anything we can understand. His peace will guard your hearts and minds as you live in Christ Jesus. (Philippians 4:6-7 NLT).

35.1 Meditation

References: Jeremiah 1:5; Luke 11:6-7; Psalm 139; Philippians 4:6-7

1. What stood out for you in this lesson?

2. What assurance do you have that God knows everything about you? Provide scriptures.

3. What is the purpose of adversity?

4. How do you handle sudden changes in your life?

5. What does it mean to despair, and why shouldn't you do it?

6. Where is God during your difficult times? Provide scriptures.

36 Dreams

In February 2014 I was getting ready for the launch of my first book, literature festival and African Heritage event titled, RÊVE.

RÊVE, the French word for dream, was a fitting title because I had been dreaming about writing a book since high school. Reminiscing on the event, and how well the book has done since publication made me think about the other dreams that I am still pregnant with. There is a set time for everything, therefore I will give birth to those dreams in due season.

It is never too late to realize your dreams. Many of the things that I conceived as a teenager are only now coming to life in my adult years. This is a testimony that it is never too late, and you are never too old to do anything you set your mind to.

When we lie down to sleep we sometimes see pictures that tell stories - stories that replay events of our previous days, or stories that speak of things to come. Many of us remember our dreams and are able to articulate them to others, while many don't remember their dreams, to the point where they conclude that they don't dream at all. I feel sad for them because I cannot imagine life without dreams.

The beauty about dreams is that we don't have to be asleep to dream. You can dream with your eyes wide open, walking on the street, laying on the couch watching television, even in the midst of a conversation with a friend. You know those thoughts you have when you zone out in the midst of a conversation with a friend? Imagining things that are not, but you would like to experience? Yes, those are dreams. They call them daydreams. It is a powerful way to use the gift of imagination that God created us with.

Your dreams (life vision) are for a set time but you have to do something so that you are moving in the direction of making them a reality. Simply thinking or talking about doing is not doing. The Scripture says, faith without works is dead. (James 2:17). You have to take deliberate steps to make a plan, then work toward making the plan a reality. Planning without taking action is a waste of time, and acting without planning is foolish.

In the book of Habakkuk the Lord told him, *"Write the vision; make it plain on tablets, so he may run who reads it"* (Habakkuk 2:2 ESV). Write down your vision or plan, then run – set out to accomplish each goal step by step. Planning is a Kingdom principle. God speaks of His plans numerous times in scripture, so when you plan, you are operating a key principle of the Kingdom of Heaven. A plan is a roadmap that tells you which direction to go in. A well laid plan that is committed to God, will move you in the right direction, no plan leads you nowhere, and a faulty plan will get you lost.

Many times God speaks to us through our dreams, but we miss out on what He is saying because we don't pay attention. For some of us, it is only when we are asleep that our spirit is quiet enough for God to get through to us. He gives us instructions or warnings through our dreams.

In Matthew chapter two God warned Joseph in a dream to flee to Egypt with the baby Jesus because Herod wanted to kill Him. The angel warned Joseph not to return until God told Him to. Later in the chapter we see that after Herod's death, the Lord spoke to Joseph in another dream and told him it was safe to go back to Israel.

In the Old Testament we read of King Nebuchadnezzar's dreams that he asked Daniel to interpret. Joseph, son of Jacob, was given a glimpse of his future in two dreams. There are numerous others who received instructions from God in their dreams.

The reason why God can do that is because He has already lived our lives and knows what is going to happen from one moment to the next. He went through it all from before the foundation of the world, therefore He knows how each of our lives will unfold. In Isaiah chapter forty six when God was reminding rebellious Israel who He was to them, He asked them this question, *"To whom will you compare me? Who is my equal?"* (verse 5).

Israel had fallen back into idol worship and God was reminding them that He is their God and there is none like Him (verse 9). He then went on to tell them:

Only I can tell you the future before it happens. Everything I plan will come to pass, for I do whatever I wish. (Isaiah 46:10 NLT).

He knows the end from the beginning. Before anything was created, He knew and determined the outcome. So Godly dreams and visions are point in time snapshots of what has already happened in eternity that will manifest at an appointed time on Earth. What an awe-full (full of awe) God! He wrote it all out in His book before the foundations of the world, then gives us nuggets of instruction, guidance and encouragement along the way to keep us focused and connected to Him while we are living out this life. What a faithful and loving Father!

Our dreams contain God's plans and purpose for our lives. He said in Jeremiah 29:11 ERV, *"I have good plans for you. I don't plan to hurt you. I plan to give you hope and a good future."*

Your dreams are potent with Divine, creative power. They are coming out of the womb of God, the Ultimate Creator. By the time you receive that dream, it is already done. All you have to do is to move in syncopation with God to see it become a reality. Be careful who you share your dreams with. There are dream killers and dream stealers lurking all around who will try to rob you of your dream and take it for themselves, dissuade you from pursuing it, or to try to kill it.

Joseph's dreams weren't things he conjured up on his own, they were God-given. God used those dreams to give him a glimpse of what God had planned for his life. You can read the story in Genesis thirty-seven. Joseph made a mistake in telling his brothers and his father about his dreams. He thought they would be happy for him, or at least help him to understand their meaning. Instead, his father, Jacob, criticized him and his brothers became jealous of him, so jealous that they sold him into slavery and told Jacob that a wild animal had killed him.

His brothers hated him and for what? For no other reason than the magnitude of his dreams. As a result of their hatred, Joseph ended up as a slave in Egypt, in Potiphar's house. While he was there Potiphar's wife accused him of sexual misconduct and Joseph was thrown in jail as a result. Do you see the damage that can be done when you share your dreams with the wrong people? Not everybody will be happy or supportive of what God is doing in your life. Not even your own family. Nevertheless, as Joseph would tell his brothers later in chapter fifty, they meant it for evil, but God meant if for good.

Rest assured that those who come against you, or try to steal or kill your dream, will fail. You may have to go through a season of hardship and isolation, but God is with you every step of the way. The very situation that they setup to destroy you, God will use it to build you and elevate you. In the end they will have to bow down to the One who gave you those dreams. They will see, that of a truth, this thing is of God.

They that rejected you, will embrace you. They that laughed at you will hang their heads in shame, because God can do anything and no one can stop His plans and purpose for your life. Be encouraged. There is more going for you than against you. Start dreaming again. If you have put your dreams aside because of what people said, go pick them up again. Get up, shake yourself out of the dust, and activate those God-given dreams NOW.

The situation does not have to be perfect for you to start. How do you eat an elephant? One bite at a time. Start small, stretch your faith and allow God to move you forward. With God all things are possible, so take the limits off and dream big!

Now GO.

36.1 Meditation

References: Genesis 37; Habakkuk 2:2; Isaiah 46:5, 9, 10; Jeremiah 29:11; Matthew 2

1. What stood out for you in this lesson?

2. Why are your dreams important?

3. What is the purpose of your dreams?

4. Why should you carefully guard your dreams?

5. How do you activate your dreams?

6. What was the importance of Joseph's dreams?

7. What are the dreams God has given you?

8. Have you made a plan or written down the vision? If not what's stopping you?

9. Do you need help in drafting your plan/vision?

37 God is in Control

I sn't it amazing how we can pull spiritual principles out of just about anything? The scripture says, *"Blessed are the pure in heart for they shall see God."* (Matthew 5:8 KJV). Notice it didn't say the pure in heart will see God at the end of their lives, or when they are happy or sad or sick. It didn't give any conditions except that their hearts are pure.

The pure in heart will see God in every situation. A pure heart will give you a godly outlook on life. One who is pure in heart sees the possibilities in every circumstance. They look for the good or best possible outcome at every turn. They know that nothing can happen in their lives without God's permission, therefore they are confident that whatever the situation, it will turn out for their good, and God will get the glory. They are always in God's business wondering what He's up to.

I don't watch a lot of television. However there are certain things that I will give my attention to. Aside from Star Trek, I derive much joy from watching home renovation shows, and of course, I have my favourite ones.

A while ago I was watching The Property Brothers, my favourite of them all. I enjoy this show for two reasons:

1. I love twins, and these twin brothers are very good at what they do, and you can tell that this is one of their natural gifting, which means,
2. They are operating in their purpose.

In this particular episode, the client was having trouble trusting Jonathan's design ideas and worried about what the end result would look like. She confessed that it was hard for her not being in control of the situation, and having to rely on someone else for the result.

Consequently, she tried to sway Jonathan into doing things her way but he wasn't having it. He said to her, "This is the way I am going to do it, and you just have to trust me that you will like the end result." (Paraphrase).

It made me think that this is how we are sometimes with the Heavenly Father. We may find it difficult to trust Him in times when things are out of our control. We may even try to take things into our own hands. Jonathan's client quickly found out that she could not coerce him into going her way. Likewise we cannot bully God or twist His arm to make things go our way. He has a Divine Design that He is working out for us and we just have to trust Him for the end result.

King Solomon said in Proverbs 19:21 ESV, *"Many are the plans in the mind of a man, but it is the purpose of the Lord that will stand."*

Who are those who fear the Lord? He will show them the path they should choose. They will live in prosperity, and their children will inherit the land. (Psalm 25:12-13 NLT).

We may have certain plans for our lives, but sooner or later we will have to put aside our agendas and come in alignment with God's plans for us. When His plans become our plans, then and only then is He in control. It can be very uncomfortable to let go and let God. However, until we do, we will not be able to live our best lives. When it gets uncomfortable and you don't know where you are going, or what to do next, know that God is up to something. He is getting ready to do something new for you.

See, I am doing a new thing! Now it springs up; do you not perceive it? I am making a way in the wilderness and streams in the wasteland. (Isaiah 43:19 NIV).

Can you trust Him to do what's best for you? Can you trust Him to reveal His Divine Design for your life?

At the end of the show the customer was pleasantly surprised at what Jonathan had done with the space. She humbly conceded that it looked terrific, and her suggestions would have been nowhere near that good. She beamed with pride and admitted that her money was well spent.

God's plan for us is way beyond anything that we can imagine. *He is able to do abundantly, exceedingly more than we can ever ask or imagine.* The Amplified Bible says, *He is able to do superabundantly, far over and above all we dare ask or think [infinitely beyond our highest prayers, desires, thoughts, hopes or dreams].* (Ephesians 3:20).

In other words God's dream for us is bigger than anything we can dream for ourselves. No matter what we think we can be or do, He can still blow our minds. So the next time you are tempted to take matters into your own hands, why not relinquish control to the One who has you in the palm of His hand?

Let go and let God.

37.1 Meditation

References: Matthew 5:8; Proverbs 19:21; Isaiah 43:19; Ephesians 3:20

1. What stood out for you in this lesson?

2. Who are the pure in heart?

3. What are some ways that we can give God control of our lives?

4. Why do we sometimes try to control our situations instead of trusting God?

5. What does it mean to trust God?

38 It's In You

W hat if I told you that everything you need to live a fulfilled, purposeful and prosperous life is inside of you? I love the Holy Spirit, and I love how he explains things to me. One night I dreamt that I was looking for a house to buy. The real estate agent and I went to look at a house that I recognize from my childhood.

The fence seemed much taller than I remembered and I was even more impressed when I went inside. There were beautiful dark hard wood floors and the house itself seemed to have been designed and constructed around a massive tree that was growing in the middle of it. The trunk of this tree was gigantic, and a key feature that improved the ambience of the house. We went back to inspect the outside and I noticed that the tall fence was only a child's drawing. The drawing was so well done, that from a certain angle it looked like the real thing.

When I woke up the Holy Spirit explained to me that the house represents me. Even though that fence was put there for security, it was only an illusion. My security is not from external sources like a fanily, career or investments. My security comes from the Source within me. That big, strong tree that was in the house was the Lord Himself on the inside of me. He alone is my Source and my security. Wow! What a visual! It is even more profound because this came at a time when I had just lost my job.

Every human being was put on Earth to fulfill a purpose. In order to fulfill our individual purpose, God deposited everything that we would need to do it in our spirits before we were born. The scripture says *He has blessed us with every spiritual blessing in Heavenly places.* (Ephesians 1:3 KJV).

Everything we need is inside us. We were not meant to live our lives separated from our Source. Our spirits should connect to the limitless Spirit that we came out of for the download of what we need moment by moment.

When someone sends us a file in a text or an email, we have to download the file in order to have access to it, but before we can even read that text or email message certain things have to be in place. First you need a device like a smartphone, computer or tablet to display the message. Then that device has to be connected to the Internet, with all the right protocols in place, in order to transact that download. In this case the Bible is our device and the Holy Spirit is our connection.

God is the Source of all good things. Therefore when your born again spirit connects to His Spirit with the protocols of faith operating in love, He will download the information directly to your spirit. Your mind then accesses your spirit in order to bring it to reality, then you make declarations in line with the revelations.

The scripture says *the tongue can speak words that bring life or death. Those who love to talk must be ready to accept what it brings.* (Proverbs 18:21 ERV). What you speak determines what you experience. Poverty is not a state of your bank account, it's a spiritual problem. What are you thinking? What are you speaking? You speak only what you believe and belief starts in the mind. You will only receive what you believe.

Do you find yourself speaking negatively about your life and situations? Do you say things like:

- I don't have any money
- I can't find a job
- I am sick

Do your sentences include a lot of I don'ts and I can'ts? If so, you need a mind and mouth transformation. You need to think and say what you want to see. Say what the word of God says:

- Wealth and riches are in my house. I may be having a cash flow problem right now, but I have abundantly, exceedingly more than I can ask or imagine. There is a surplus of [*amount*] in my bank account.

- I have a job – the right job for me, because it was supplied before the foundations of the world. I may not know where it is, but the Lord leads me in the path that I should take. He has already opened the door and is leading me to walk through it.
- By His stripes I am healed. Even if the situation doesn't look good. I walk by faith and not by sight. God said it, I believe it and it is so.

The world is in a bad state because they refuse to acknowledge the true and living God. World Governments can't solve the world's problems. It's not because they are not educated or intelligent, but the world needs more than human intelligence to fix its problems. It needs a Higher Government; one that is outside the realm of where their problems lie.

The world's biggest problem is spiritual bankruptcy, and until the wealth of revelatory knowledge that exists in the Kingdom of God is deposited back into the spirits of humanity, the world will continue to run a deficit.

My people are destroyed for lack of knowledge. Because you have rejected knowledge, I also will reject you from being my priest. Since you have forgotten the law of your God, I also will forget your children. (Hosea 4:6 NIV).

This verse is not talking about the knowledge that comes from Ivy League education. It is talking about a Higher Learning of the spiritual or divine dimension. Human beings are powerful because of how we were created. We were pulled right out of the Spirit of God, so the unregenerate human still has a level of power within himself. Notice how some unbelievers prosper? It's because they have studied, tapped into and are applying certain universal laws that God put in place.

Remember that God causes his rain to fall on the just and the unjust. So as long as you believe and are operating His principles in love, you will see the benefits. Yet there is even more power available to us when we allow the Spirit of Christ to possess our spirits. When we cooperate with Him, we give way for abundantly, exceedingly more to come in and change our world. He knows where the hidden treasures are. That includes, jobs, money, spouse and other divine relationships, homes, whatever you need.

So the next time you are tempted to fall into negativity, or look outside you for what you need, run to the word of God and get His view about your situation. Find the word that fits your circumstances and meditate on it until it fills you up, and when life's pressures show up to squeeze you, only the word will be spilling out of you.

Declare the Word over your situation. The revelations will come that will instruct you how to change the situation. God spoke and created the universe. We have that same power to create, so speak and create your world. Draw from the divine Source of life within you and speak what you want to see in your life.

It's in you.

38.1 Meditation

References: Proverbs 18:21; Hosea 4:6; Ephesians 1:3, 3:20

1. What stood out for you in this lesson?

2. List some scriptures with explanations, where it speaks about our purpose.

3. What is in you that will help you navigate life?

4. How do you access what's in you?

5. Poverty is a _____. Explain with scriptures.

6. What is that power that is at work in born again believers?

7. How does it differ from the power in unbelievers?

8. Why are some unbelievers able to fulfill their life's purpose?

9. Why don't some believers fulfill their life's purpose?

10. What should you do when you are tempted to fall into negativity?

39 Loyalty

L oyalty: Faithfulness to commitments or obligations; Faithful adherence to a Sovereign, government, leader or cause.

A few years ago I was having a discussion with someone about car insurance. In recent years car insurance has increased significantly and depending on where you live in Canada, you could be paying a hefty sum monthly or yearly. Such was my discussion with the lady who explained that she really wants to purchase a property in a particular neighbourhood, but was hesitant based on the fact that her car insurance premiums would increase if she did.

My insurance company is not necessarily the most inexpensive of the bunch but I chose to remain loyal to them over the years because of how they have treated me in the past. About ten years ago I went through a financially challenging period that resulted in my car insurance being cancelled. The owner of the franchise did something memorable. She was nine months pregnant and on bed rest per Doctor's orders and left her mother in charge of the business. On learning of the cancellation, her mom phoned her at home and informed her of it.

The owner went against Doctor's orders, got out of bed and went into the office to do battle on my behalf. I was later told of her conversation with their head office which went something like this:

"This woman has been a faithful customer all these years. If she is late with her payments there must be a reason. Have you looked at her file and seen her track record? I am not going back home until you reverse that decision and give her some time to sort out her situation. I don't care what you have to do. Etc., etc., etc."

Suffice it to say she got her way and my personal situation was sorted out not long afterwards and things went back to normal. I stay loyal to that insurance company because of her sacrifice for me, not because of the conglomerate. For despite the fact that I had been doing things by the book in the past, one deviation is all it took for them to cut me off.

I say that to say this. We all have our favourite brands, people, teams, etc. that we are loyal to for different reasons. But how loyal are we to the Creator and our Heavenly Father – the One who created us, provides for us, protects us, does battle for us?

He gave His only begotten who became a sacrifice for our redemption, to bring us back into our position as His children. Knowing that someone died in our place should be enough of a reason to be loyal or faithful to Him, but if that does not do it for you, look what Psalm 103: 2-5 NIV says.

*Praise the L*ORD*, my soul, and forget not all his benefits—³ who forgives all your sins and heals all your diseases, ⁴ who redeems your life from the pit and crowns you with love and compassion, ⁵ who satisfies your desires with good things so that your youth is renewed like the eagle's.*

That entire chapter is a sobering account of who God is, who He is to us and what He does for us.

So while we place loyalty in things here on earth, let us remember to also place our loyalty where it is most deserving; to the One above.

For *"…from everlasting to everlasting the L*ORD*'s love is with those who fear him, and his righteousness with their children's children—¹⁸ with those who keep his covenant and remember to obey his precepts." (vv17-18).*

Let us place our loyalty where the benefits are everlasting for even if we make a mistake, He will not cut us off. In those times He extends His grace to us and surrounds us with His love. When we correct the mistake by repenting, it will be turned around for our good and God's glory.

Where are you placing your loyalty?

39.1 Meditation

References: Psalm 103

1. What stood out for you in this lesson?

2. What does loyalty mean to you?

3. Why should we be loyal to our Heavenly Father?

4. What are the benefits that God blesses us with? Provide scriptures.

5. Explain the meaning of 'your youth is renewed like an Eagle's'.

6. What other scriptures speak about the enduring love of God?

7. In your own words explain the covenants of God.

40 Passion

I t was a beautiful Saturday. The weather was just superb with bright, golden sunshine and the welcome warmth of spring preparing us for summer. Yes! I was thinking about summer even while enduring the fickle volatility of the spring weather.

I enjoyed the day immensely. It was one of those personally quiet days that I luxuriate in. At some point during the day I got to thinking about being authentically unique, operating in purpose and being true to who I am. I read somewhere that when you find something in life worth dying for you have found your passion, and that passion leads you to discovering purpose.

As I meditated it hit me. I cannot be in purpose and be immobile or stagnant. Purpose is designed to push you forward. Purpose compels you to act – to do something with or about that passion. Then I thought, "what am I willing to die for?" I can certainly list two or three things that I am passionate about, but am I willing to die for all of those things? My answer came quickly and was more of a confirmation than a discovery.

Keeping this in perspective I thought of one person who died to fulfill purpose. Jesus. He believed so strongly in what He came to earth to do that He willingly gave His life for it.

But he replied, "I must preach the Good News of the Kingdom of God in other towns, too, because that is why I was sent. (Luke 4:43-44 NLT).

While operating in purpose He faced severe opposition, was hated, criticized, rejected, you name it. It didn't stop Him from doing what He came to do. He was operating authentically, influencing the world around Him and having a great impact on his community. This caused polarization among the masses; some loved Him, some hated Him. He believed so strongly in His convictions that He died for them.

This tells me a few things:

1. You have to be authentic (know and be true to who you are) to operate effectively in your purpose.
2. You have to believe in yourself and have a sincere conviction about what you were given to do.
3. When all hell comes against you, push forward. Opposition comes when you are headed in the right direction.
4. Be prepared to go alone if that's what it takes.
5. There is great sacrifice involved in fulfilling purpose – sometimes to the point of death.

What are you passionate about? What are you doing about it? Are you willing to die for it?

40.1 Meditation

Reference: Luke 4:43-44

1. What stood out for you in this lesson?

2. What does it mean to be passionate about something?

3. What are you passionate about?

4. Do you see your life's purpose in it? And are you willing to die for it?

5. Are you acting on those promptings of purpose? If no, why not?

6. What is the meaning of influence?

41 Role Models

I like people. There are even a few that I admire. When I was younger there were those that I used to hold up as role models. Do you still do that? I selected them as role models because of some qualities that stood out about them that I wanted to emulate.

Maybe it was the way they dressed, spoke, or some memorable act that they did. I cautiously maintain that concept in my life because some of those who I saw in that light turned into major disappointments. They became drug addicts, ended up in prison or just never lived up to the hype. They had deficiencies and could not sustain the image that initially made me want to be like them. I say this on the heels of being awarded the 2016 Role Models Award by a Canadian organization earlier this year.

I once wrote a blog that said none of us have to imitate another human being and that is true. When God made us he gave us His nature. If you have God's nature why would you want to imitate someone that is merely human?

Read what Romans 8: 8-9 NKJV says, *So then, those who are in the flesh cannot please God. ⁹ But you are not in the flesh but in the Spirit, if indeed the Spirit of God dwells in you. Now if anyone does not have the Spirit of Christ, he is not His.*

A mere human being is someone who does not have the Spirit of God. God's nature is spirit. When He made man, He made a spirit-being but man lost His spiritual connection to God through sin in the Garden of Eden. When Adam and Eve sinned the spiritual connection was severed, and they lost dominion over the Earth to satan. Not long afterwards God recalled His Spirit out of the Earth. (Genesis 6:3).

Christ came to restore what was lost and through His Spirit we were reconciled to God as sons. Whether you are male or female you are a son. Your gender is given to you to function in the earth, but you are first and foremost a spirit-being. God is the father of spirits, not flesh (Hebrews 12:9), so in the spirit, you are a son (John 1:12).

When God made us he gave us His nature. God is a Spirit, therefore His nature is Spirit. If you have God's nature (spirit) why would you want to be like anybody else? Be careful who, or what, you are trying to measure up to. You may be lowering your value. Why would you want to be like someone who is not operating by the Spirit of Christ? Why would you want me as a role model if I am not rightly representing Christ?

The Apostle Paul said, "Follow me, as I follow Christ." Or, follow my example, as I follow Christ's example. Yet another translation writes it as, imitate me, as I imitate Christ. (1 Corinthians 11:1).

Before you try to imitate anyone, find out who He created you to be and become that person. Who are you? You were created for a purpose therefore you were uniquely equipped with certain gifts and talents to fulfill that purpose.

"Before I formed you in the womb I knew you; before you were born I sanctified you; I ordained you a prophet to the nations." (Jeremiah 1:5 NKJV).

God knew you before you were born and he ordained you to do something unique in the earth. Your personality and your gifts and talents were uniquely designed for your assignment. Get to know the real you, and find your gifts and talents and let God show you how to use them for His glory. Find out what your purpose is and rock it!

Remember, you are unique and special because you were created that way. Allow God to develop His character in you and help you to grow to become more like Christ. Before you try to emulate me or anyone else, let Him make you over into the best version of you.

Make Christ your first and ultimate role model and learn to be authentically you.

41.1 Meditation

Reference: Romans 8:8-9; Genesis 6:3, Hebrews 12:9; John 1:12, 1 Corinthians 11:1; Jeremiah 1:5

1. What stood out for you this lesson?

2. Who is a true role model? Provide scriptures.

3. What are the privileges of having the Spirit of Christ?

4. What does it mean to have God's nature? Provide scriptures.

5. Why should you be careful who you choose as a role model?

6. Who would your ideal role model be?

7. Are you living in such a way to be a positive influence to someone else?

8. Who are you authentically?

42 Stepping in the Right Direction

We often pray and ask God to direct our steps. Understand that as a part of that He will also direct your stops. You may be engaged in activities thinking it is what the Lord wants you to do, but somewhere along the way you realize that you are not making any progress. We know that we get opposition from the enemy of our souls so that goes without saying.

However there are times when you have to pause and ask yourself a couple of questions:

• Have I approached this correctly?
• Is this really what I am supposed to be doing?

If you know beyond a shadow of a doubt that the answer to these questions is in the affirmative, then there may be other reasons for the lack of progress. Are you hindering yourself?

There are times that Daddy has put a stop order on that thing because it is not the right time for it or that is not what He wants you to do in this season. Or it may be the right season but you are approaching it with the wrong mindset. When He orders a stop it is because He is directing you to do something else, or go somewhere else. He is directing your steps in a different direction.

So if you are in a place where nothing seems to be working, and you are not sure what to do or how to proceed, remember that when you don't know the next step, you always know the One who directs your steps. He knows the end from the beginning and He knows the path that you should take.

If you want to know what God wants you to do, ask him, and he will gladly tell you, for he is always ready to give a bountiful supply of wisdom to all who ask him; he will not resent it. (James 1:5 TLB)

Ask Him for direction.

42.1 Meditation

Reference: James 1:5

1. What stood out for you in this lesson?

2. What are some reasons that things may not be working out as we would hope?

3. What should you do in those situations?

4. What are some scriptures that speak about God directing our lives?

5. What role does wisdom play in all this?

6. How can a person hinder their own progress?

43 Stop Struggling

E ver heard this quote? "About the time we think we can make ends meet, somebody moves the ends."

I first saw this quote on a plaque that was hanging on the living room wall of an acquaintance a few years ago. It was spoken by past US President Herbert Hoover, and has become a part of pop culture. Every so often I hear someone repeat it when they are dealing with a stressful situation, usually a financial one.

It seems like no matter how hard you work and apply your financial acumen things just never seem to add up. Then you wonder, "what am I working for?" At times you feel despondent and want to throw in the towel and call it quits, but I encourage you to hang on and stay strong. Your situation is not unique.

In the Luke 5:1-7, a group of men had the same issue and they called it quits...at least for the day. But that didn't last for long. They came in contact with someone who could provide the solution to their problem. It was just what they needed.

> One day as Jesus was preaching on the shore of the Sea of Galilee, great crowds pressed in on him to listen to the word of God. ² He noticed two empty boats at the water's edge, for the fishermen had left them and were washing their nets. ³ Stepping into one of the boats, Jesus asked Simon, its owner, to push it out into the water. So he sat in the boat and taught the crowds from there.

KARLENE MILLWOOD

4 When he had finished speaking, he said to Simon, "Now go out where it is deeper, and let down your nets to catch some fish."

5 "Master," Simon replied, "we worked hard all last night and didn't catch a thing. But if you say so, I'll let the nets down again." 6 And this time their nets were so full of fish they began to tear! 7 A shout for help brought their partners in the other boat, and soon both boats were filled with fish and on the verge of sinking. (Luke 5:1-7 NLT).

Working hard doesn't always get us the results or returns that we want. That is why we have to learn to trust our Heavenly Father to meet our needs. Peter struggled to catch fish all night but when he surrendered his vessel, the symbol of his work, to Jesus, his struggles ceased.

Another way to look at it is that he invested of his substance into Jesus' ministry and activated the laws of seedtime and harvest. When you are in lack and give God what is in your hands, He will always give you back *good measure, pressed down, shaken together and running over.* (Luke 6:38 NLT).

Though he was hesitant at first, Peter followed Jesus' instructions and it became easy to do what he struggled to do earlier. He caught an overflow – an abundance of fish that was enough to serve himself and his partners, to the point where the boats almost sank. When we give our substance to Jesus to use it for His purposes, He will always return to us more than we gave Him. He multiplies it then gives it back to us. He always does more than we expect – abundantly, exceedingly more. Just learn to take Him at His word and obey His instructions.

Are you ready to stop struggling?

43.1 Meditation

References: Luke 5:1-7; Luke 6:38

1. What stood out for you in this lesson?

2. What does it mean to struggle (biblically)?

3. How can we stop struggling?

4. How do Psalm 95:11 and Hebrews 3:11 relate to this lesson?

5. What is the law of seedtime and harvest? Provide scriptures.

6. When we give God what we have, what does He do?

7. What other law are we activating in the question above?

8. What was Peter struggling with in this lesson? How did he overcome it?

44 Talking To Strangers

R emember when we were kids and our parents told us not to talk to strangers? Obeying this rule likely kept us out of many harmful and dangerous situations. In this time when online luring of teenagers into prostitution and other compromising situations is so prevalent, this is sound advice.

Though this is valid in childhood, this same principle does not always bode well in adulthood. As we go about our daily lives we encounter countless numbers of people that we don't know on a train, in an elevator, at a restaurant...you get the drift. We greet and sometimes engage in conversations with some of these individuals, some of whom we become close to over time. Yes, there are those occasions when we come across some unsavoury characters, but most of us have learnt how to extricate ourselves from those situations.

I met a young lady while working on a project a few years ago. She was very quiet and unassuming but pleasant. Although she didn't say much she always had a hint of a smile on her face and that attracted me to her. I decided to break the ice one day by introducing myself to her. We chatted briefly and from that moment it became easier for her to greet me when she saw me. The relationship did not develop beyond hellos so essentially we remained strangers of a sort to each other.

Recently I came to a crossroads in my career. I knew it was time for a change but I didn't make any rush decisions. I took time to pray and seek the Lord and sought advice from those closest to me. I was at the subway station one morning late last year when out of the corner of my eye I saw someone walking toward me. I turned around to see the beautiful smile of this young lady as she said, "Hi, how are you? I haven't seen you in a while."

We exchanged pleasantries and got to chatting about our different careers. She shared her aspirations with me and I shared my situation with her. She looked at me intently and said, "Hmmm. Seems like you need a change. Listen my boyfriend is a recruiter. Why don't I give you his contact information and you can talk to him about helping you to find what you are looking for?"

The short version of the story is that I contacted her boyfriend, the recruiter, who sent me a job posting from an organization whose account was not even handled by his company. I was called for an interview and within three weeks I was offered a new position which started the first Monday of the new year.

I look back at this with wonder and amazement at how God works. This was all His setup. I first had to be assigned to the project two years earlier in order to meet this young woman. Then I had to make contact with her, and even though we didn't become best of friends, the interaction was enough to bring about God's purpose.

I cannot help but think about the scripture that says, *"Don't forget to show hospitality to strangers, for some who have done this have entertained angels without realizing it!"* (Hebrews 13:2 NLT).

I would say I entertained my angel who brought me my breakthrough at the time when I needed it. How many times have we blocked our blessing by:

- Sidestepping that stranger who approached us?
- Thinking we were better than someone and so refused to speak to them?
- Dismissing another because they didn't sound educated or have the image of someone you want in your space?

Moral of the story: Be careful how you treat people. The one you mistreat may be the one who came with your breakthrough.

44.1 Meditation

References: Hebrews 13:2

1. What stood out for you in this lesson?

2. What biblical characters met people who were instrumental in their promotion?

3. Why should we entertain, or show hospitality, to strangers?

4. Why is it important to always be kind to others?

5. How do you feel about talking to strangers?

45 Thankfulness or Gratefulness

S anjeev jogged up the stairs to the tracks at exactly 7:10 AM, timing it precisely so that the train would be pulling into the station at the same time as he arrived. This was his usual routine so that he would spend a minimum amount of time outside in the frigid cold air of the Canadian winter mornings.

This morning was different. There was a delay because five minutes had gone by since he arrived on the platform and still no train. The other passengers around him were becoming anxious and rightly so. With the wind chill, the temperature was a bone chilling minus thirty degrees and his toes were starting to freeze in his shoes. He wished now that he had worn his warmer boots. Pulling his hood over his head, he stuffed his gloved hands deep into his pockets and hunched his shoulders against the cold.

He watched a young lady who stood close to the edge of the platform, occasionally peering around the other waiting passengers to see if she could spot the train coming in the distance.

"It's there," she said. "It's sitting on the tracks up there but it doesn't seem to be moving."

Every so often she looked and reported back. "There must be a problem. It has been sitting there for a while now."

The passengers waited another ten minutes and one by one they moved back inside the terminal. It was just too cold to continue waiting outdoors. The interior of the station was jam packed with morning commuters as those taking the later trains started to arrive. His toes now felt numb so Sanjeev decided to go back to his car and warm up.

Sliding into the driver's seat he immediately turned up the heat to maximum. As he sat there he began to pray. "Lord, thank you that you know all things. You know what is causing the delay with the train so thank you for sending your angel to fix it. In Jesus' Name. Amen."

He chuckled to himself at how shocked some people were when they found out that he believed in Jesus. Most automatically assumed that he was Hindu or Muslim because of his name; Sanjeev Acharya. Forty five minutes later the train limped into the station. Sanjeev remained in his car, watching to see what would happen. After taking on passengers the train slowly rolled away on its journey to Union Station.

He got out of the car and walked back toward the track to be in time for the one coming after. A minute later the other train pulled into the station and passengers impatiently shouldered their way on. It was standing room only as the doors closed and the train glided out of the station, but not even a minute later, it stopped abruptly.

"Ladies and gentlemen, we have a frozen switch situation ahead of us and our Engineer has gone out to manually fix it. It will be just two more minutes and we will be on our way. Again, we apologize for the inconvenience this morning." The conductor announced ruefully.

Passengers reacted in various ways to this. Some sighed deeply and heavily while others complained loudly. Sanjeev was determined to be different. He silently prayed, "Lord, let me see you in this."

A few minutes later thoughts started flowing through his mind. As he focused on the thoughts he realized that God had answered his prayer to let him find some good in the situation. Sanjeev smiled and said a silent hallelujah. Although the situation was unpleasant there were a lot of positive things that one could take away if they thought correctly.

Sanjeev thought, "It is freezing cold but at least I can feel it. Thank you Lord that I am alive and healthy and able to be up and about on this cold day. Although these people are unhappy and complaining, I can hear them. Thank you for the ability to hear. Some people were born without the ability to hear and speak. Some lost it along the way but mine is still intact. I am on my way to work while there are thousands of people worldwide who don't have, or never had a job.

Thank you Lord that I know you and because of that I can choose my response to this situation. Thank you for wisdom. Even though we are delayed I am on a train. There are those who have to walk miles and miles to work. Thank you for my car and for public transportation."

Sanjeev let the thoughts flow through him and for each positive thing he continued to silently give God thanks. He remembered the scripture in 1 Thessalonians 5:18 TLB which says *"No matter what happens, always be thankful, for this is God's will for you who belong to Christ Jesus."*

Remember that there is purpose in everything that happens in life and no matter what you are facing, there is always something to give thanks for. Keep that in your thoughts as you go through your day and this week. Have a fabulous day full of wonder and God's blessings.

45.1 Meditation

Reference: 1 Thessalonians 5:18

1. What stood out for you in this lesson?

2. Why should we always be thankful?

3. List some benefits of thanksgiving.

4. What other scriptures speak about thanksgiving or being thankful?

5. What does it mean to see God in a situation?

46 Whose Report will You Believe?

Dentist appointments are annoying but necessary for me. I don't know what turns me off more, the ugly tools that dentists use or the nerve racking sounds that they make, or the constant lectures about brushing and flossing every day. We all brush every day, at least I hope so, but let's face it, we don't all floss on a daily basis. Do you? Well, if you do, you are better than me.

Whenever I have to visit my dentist I go with trepidation fully expecting the dooms day homily that that I always hear. "You have beautiful teeth, my dear, but you should pull this or do that because if you don't then…" Some negative thing is always going to happen. I usually just respond with "Right. I hear you…see you next time." I can never get away fast enough to sit in my car and breathe that sigh of relief.

My last two appointments have been interesting. My regular Dentist has been busy so on the first of these two visits, I saw the Head Dentist and owner of the business. While working on my teeth all I heard him saying was, "You have beautiful teeth. You do a good job of keeping them healthy. Well done."

I could hardly believe my ears! Surely the Head Dentist is going to take me to task for not caring enough about my teeth! Hmmm…maybe he is just a nice guy. Well, on the second of these visits my Dentist was again busy so I saw the Hygienist. Guess what she said.

"You have beautiful teeth. Very nice. Do you brush and floss often?" Ha! So much for that Dr. Dentist! I am still not flossing every day but yes I brush often. So what is all this? Do I just feel like telling you my dentistry woes?

No, there is a reason for it. This whole scenario got me thinking about the different types of messages we get interacting with people daily and how important it is to filter the information that we take in. Whatever you take in is going to impact you negatively or positively. The book of Proverbs tells us how to deal with this.

Guard your heart above all else, for it determines the course of your life. (Proverbs 4:23 NLT).

We are living in the Information Age so we are deluged with information daily and sometimes it can be overwhelming. Be careful what you allow to get inside of you and to stay. Guard your heart diligently and think good thoughts. Forgive quickly and love regardless.

A negative heart produces a negative life and a positive heart produces a positive life. So I encourage you to guard your heart and decide whose report to believe. It goes without saying that I believe the Head Dentist and the Hygienist in this case. Always believe the positive.

"You cannot have a positive life and a negative mind" (Joyce Meyer).

Whose report will you believe?

46./ Meditation

1. What stood out for you in this lesson?

2. Why is it important to guard your heart?

3. Where do the spiritual battles take place?

4. List some scriptures that tell us how to overcome these battles.

5. What happens if you think negatively?

6. How can negative thinking be corrected? Explain.

KARLENE MILLWOOD

47 The Necessity of Pruning

G od prunes our lives of things that are not good for us. *He cuts off every branch in me that bears no fruit, while every branch that does bear fruit he prunes so that it will be even more fruitful.* (John 15:2 NLT).

The purpose of pruning is to remove what is dead, damaged or diseased from a flower or tree, and prevent decay and ultimately death to the plant. Pruning stimulates growth and productivity. Gardeners prune plants to help them blossom, grow stronger and fuller, and bear more fruit. We are God's garden - His cultivated field, His vineyard. (1 Corinthians 3:9). Like every good gardener, God tends to His garden and does seasonal pruning in our lives so that we can grow and become more like Christ.

God works against the natural to bring out the supernatural. He uses adversity, conflicts and hardships as pruning tools in our lives. Difficulties are meant to make us, not break us, but the making is completely dependent on your cooperation with God's pruning process. Will you yield to it or resist it? What's being removed during this pruning process? Anything that does not look like Christ. Therefore old mindsets, bad habits and attitudes and anything else that may cause you to become stagnant and unfruitful is being cut away.

God removes anything that causes you to be weak, and inhibits you from moving forward and being productive and prosperous. This includes unhealthy relationships. Scripture tells us that we must love each other. Yet we must be careful how we interpret and apply this principle in our lives. There are those who will tell us that if we choose not to associate with some people we are not walking in love. It is a lie and we must be careful of that spirit.

Paul, in the book of Corinthians, tells us *that bad company corrupts good character.* (1 Corinthians 15:33 NLT). Another scripture warns us that *two cannot walk together unless they agree.* (Amos 3:3 NLT). King Solomon imparts, *Good people are careful about choosing their friends, but evil people always choose the wrong ones.* (Proverbs 12:26 ERV).

General Collin Powell said, "The less you associate with some people, the better off you are. If you run with wolves you will learn how to howl, but if you associate with eagles, you will learn how to soar to great heights."

Letting go of people doesn't mean you hate them. You can still seize the opportunities to greet and have conversations with them, however they are not allowed in your inner circle. When you prune or cut away dried branches from the flowers and trees in your home or garden, do you put them back on later? So why continue to hold on when God removes (prunes) people from your life?

When we try to hold on to what God has removed, or is removing, we are not walking in love. To love God is to obey Him. Holding on to what He has pruned is disobeying Him, and when we are disobedient, we are not walking in love toward God. Is it better to please people and displease God? Wouldn't you rather please God regardless of who is offended? God wants to use your life and His pruning process is getting you ready for the great destiny He has prepared for you. Therefore you can't run with everyone.

Building relationships is important. We are not created to walk through life alone. However we should carefully and prayerfully choose our friends. You always want those who will lead you to do what is right and inspire you to keep going higher. Be careful of who is speaking into your life. What seeds are they planting? Seeds produce a harvest. What do you want to reap? Are they building you up or tearing you down?

As I am writing this lesson, I received a text from a friend with the following words, "Keep people in your life that truly love you, motivate you, encourage you, inspire you, enhance you, and make you happy." I love when the Lord validates me. Don't you? If those around you are not doing what is in this paragraph, you must let them go. You have to set and maintain healthy boundaries to effectively walk the path that God has mapped out for you. Not everyone is meant to walk that path with you.

The Bible commands us to love our neighbours as ourselves (Mark 12:31). If you don't love yourself, you will not be able to love others. Entertaining unhealthy relationships around you can become toxic to your life, and when you do that you are not loving yourself. It is important to know that God never sends anyone in our lives to cause us stress. He is the God of peace and order. Therefore if anyone is in your life that is causing stress and confusion, they were not planted there by God and they must be uprooted and put away. Do not tolerate drama in your life unless it is on a theatrical stage or film screen.

There must be separation before elevation, so even though it may be painful, submit to God's pruning process and let Him remove everything and everyone that would weigh you down or trip you up, so you can run your race freely.

47.1 Meditation

References: John 15:2; 1 Corinthians 3:9, 15:33; Amos 3:3; Proverbs 12:26; Mark 12:31; Hebrews 12:1-2

1. What stood out for you in this lesson?

2. Explain the purpose of pruning.

3. How has God been pruning your life?

4. What does it mean to walk in love?

5. Describe the differences between a healthy and a toxic relationship.

6. Make a list of your relationships and identify which category each fits in.

7. What does it mean to love yourself?

8. Identify some areas in yourself or your life that you would like God to prune.

9. Now pray and ask Him to prune them.

48 Jealousy

I was putting the finishing touches on one of my poems one day. As I was writing I realized that my sentiments closely mirrored a status that I read on Facebook that day from T. D. Jakes.

He wrote, "You must realize that if you are going to reach the heights you have been called to reach, you may elicit some criticism from those who are jealous, petty or angry because they were left behind."

Instantly a bell went off in my head and I was reminded of a time when I was guilty of that. I am at a place in my faith walk where I have experienced jealousy on both sides; I have been jealous of others and others have been jealous of me. I remember a time many years ago when I felt jealous and angry because I didn't seem to be growing as fast as I would like spiritually. It was exactly as Bishop Jakes wrote - I was jealous of my friends who *seemed* to be making spiritual strides and leaving me in the dust.

It was an ugly, miserable feeling. I allowed the devil to wreak havoc on my mind with this until I read in the scripture that, *there is therefore now no condemnation to them which are in Christ Jesus, who do not walk according to the flesh but according to the spirit.* (Romans 8:1 NKJV).

I digested this verse of scripture and really let it get a hold of my heart. I began to accept where I was in my growth, and whenever I noticed something that I wanted to change I would bring it to the Lord and ask Him to change me within. Soon those negative emotions were nowhere to be found. I began to see the results. I was growing in the spirit and no longer felt small and insignificant. I trusted that He who began a good work in me would complete it and continued to surrender to Him.

So what is jealousy really? There are three words that can be used interchangeably to describe the same emotion: Jealous, envious and covetous.

According to dictionary.com, **jealousy** is a feeling of resentment against someone because of that person's rivalry, success, or advantages.

Envy is a feeling of discontent or covetousness with regard to another's advantages, success or possessions.

To **covet** is to desire wrongfully, inordinately, or without due regard for the rights of others.

The scripture tells us very clearly to not covet our neighbour's possessions. (Exodus 20:17). In the book of Hebrews, the writer also cautions us not to covet but to be satisfied with what we have. (Hebrews 13:5).

Jealousy is a clear indication that purpose is not known. Where purpose is not known, you will usually find jealousy and competition. When you know your purpose, you know that no one can take your place, or occupy your space, in this world.

We all have different callings on our lives, and the journey will be different for each of us. It was King David who said, *"Lord, you alone are my inheritance, my cup of blessing. You guard all that is mine. The land you have given me is a pleasant land. What a wonderful inheritance!"* (Psalm 16:5-6 NLT).

When you have knowledge of what your land (purpose, assignment) is, you won't need to cross the boundary lines and trespass onto your neighbour's land out of jealousy. People who don't know their purpose compete with each other for positions, status and things. Be reminded that God has a place for you and a pace for you to get there, so no need to envy anyone.

Jealousy is rooted in selfishness and pride, and if it is not curtailed, can be damaging to the lives of those involved. James tells us that jealousy leads to disorder and evil works, so it must be stomped out before it grows up to produce undesirable fruit. (James 3:16). Do not fight people for their positions or possessions, or try to take on activities that others are successful in. They have the grace and anointing for what they are doing, you may not. It is the anointing on them that enables them to do what they do. If you step into that place without the anointing you will fail. Be led by the Spirit.

Seek God and let Him reveal your purpose to you. In that same Psalm, King David said, *"I will bless the Lord who guides me; even at night my heart instructs me."* (v7).

God is always speaking so put yourself in a position to hear Him. He will tell you what to do and which way to go. He wants to direct your life, and His direction will lead you into the place that was pre-ordained for you before the foundations of the world. David continued by saying, *"You will show me the way of life, granting me the joy of your Presence."* (v11). When you allow God to do the leading you will always be successful. He will show you the path to take and you are guaranteed His presence. He will never leave you nor forsake you.

Joseph's brothers were jealous of him because Joseph was their father's favourite. Their jealousy caused evil to grow up in their hearts to the point where they conspired together and sold him into slavery in Egypt. Little did they know that God would use this evil act for their own good later on.

Saul became jealous of David when he heard the women singing, *Saul has slain his thousands, and David his tens of thousands. Saul looked at David with suspicion [and jealously] from that day forward."* (1 Samuel 18:7, 9 AMP). From that moment Saul turned against David and tried to kill him.

Jealousy is a fruit of the flesh. Love is not jealous or boastful or proud, therefore if you find jealousy in your heart, it means you have stepped out of love and into flesh. Repent and get rid of it quickly. Do not allow satan to use your heart and your mind to carry out his evil plans. Be thankful for your life and where you are right now. God makes no mistakes and He knows how to get you to where you are supposed to be. Don't waste your precious time being envious of others, or coveting what they have or do. It will always lead you down a wrong path.

When you trust God to direct your life, He will always lead you in the path that is right. Examine yourself and be sure to walk in love, and let the peace of God rule in your heart.

48.1 Meditation

References: Romans 8:1; Exodus 20:17; Hebrews 13:5; Psalm 16; James 3:16; 1 Corinthians 13:4; Genesis 29, 37

1. What stood out for you in this lesson?

2. What is jealousy?

3. What other emotions can it be compared with?

4. Why should we not harbor these emotions in our hearts?

5. Think for a moment. Is there anyone that you are jealous of right now?

6. If so, what can you do to change that?

7. What is the relationship between jealousy and purpose?

8. What attitude or emotion is at the root of jealousy?

9. What are some of the things jealousy can cause you to do?

10. How does jealousy relate to the fruits of the Spirit?

11. What is the best way to overcome the emotion of jealousy?

49 Are you a Victim or a Victor?

I was on the train to work one morning and was reflecting on my life in these past few years. I thought about some things that I had been through and how I went through them. Some of them I handled well and felt good about myself afterwards. Others I did not do as well and felt defeated and beaten up when all was said and done.

I learned a lot from these situations. I realize that how I view life's challenges will determine how I handle them, and how I handle them will determine the end result. Will it be positive or negative?

We go through many struggles, trials, and adversities in our lifetime. When we view them as things that are happening to us (negative) instead of for us (positive), we are likely to go through them feeling defeated.

When we look at these situations from the perspective that they are happening to us, we can easily develop a victim mentality. However, if we see them as happening for us we are more likely to go through them victoriously.

Romans 8: 28-29 NLT says, *and we know that in all things God works for the good of those who love Him, who have been called according to his purpose. For those God knew He also predestined to be conformed to the image of his Son, that He might be the firstborn among many brothers and sisters.*

When we believe that all things are working together for our good it's a powerful thing. We will begin to stretch our thinking to ask questions like:

- What am I supposed to learn from this?
- How should I respond to this?
- Is there something in me that needs to change?

The moment we begin to look at the situation from this place, or ask these simple questions, we have positioned ourselves to go through the situation in peace. Guaranteed we are coming out stronger, wiser and ready to teach someone else.

But thank God! He has made us Hs captives and continues to lead us along in Christ's triumphal procession. Now He uses us to spread the knowledge of Christ everywhere, like a sweet perfume
(2 Corinthians 2:14 NLT).

49.1 Meditation

References: Romans 8:28-29; 2 Corinthians 2:14

1. What stood out for you in this lesson?

2. Think of some things you've been through. Write down the ones where you were victorious and the ones where you failed?

3. How did you feel when you were:

   a. Victorious

   b. Failed

4. What role does perspective play in the outcome of life's challenges?

5. Explain the victim mentality in your own words.

6. What is the mindset of a victor?

7. How will this information help you to go through future challenges?

50 Loving Through the Pain

I t is said that the only constant in life is change. We have to change in order to grow. Growth is necessary for success, but changing and growing is painful. Consider a pregnant mother how she may feel as her body stretches and adjusts to fit the growing baby inside her. Not to diminish the gestation experience, but consider that your dreams and visions are the baby that you are pregnant with.

Just as that mother's body changes to allow her baby to grow in preparation for birth, you must also grow in order for your dreams and visions to manifest. God will allow us to experience hardships to stretch us. He has to expand our capacity and strengthen us for the next level. In the book of Isaiah, the prophet exhorts the children of Israel to rejoice in anticipation of giving birth when they came out of exile. But they had to make some preparation for this future expansion of their families.

In verse two of chapter fifty four he tells them, *"Enlarge the site of your tent [to make room for more children]; Stretch out the curtains of your dwellings, do not spare them; Lengthen your tent ropes and make your pegs (stakes) firm [in the ground]. For you will spread out to the right and to the left.* (Isaiah 54: 2-3a AMP).

Israel had to expand their homes for the increased capacity of individuals that would join their ranks and increase their numbers. They were about to burst forth at the seams and had to be ready to manage the additional influx of souls to their nation. Likewise we have to be prepared to handle our next level and the preparation often comes with some uncomfortable and painful shifts and changes in our lives. Every level comes with its own

KARLENE MILLWOOD

challenges, and we have to be strengthened mentally, emotionally and spiritually to face what lies ahead of us.

Change happens in many ways. It could be the loss of a job, an illness or loss of key relationships through death or separation. However it happens, it can be painful. In these situations we have to learn to think differently and do things differently to cope. The scripture says, *"If you fall to pieces during a crisis, there wasn't much to you in the first place."* (Proverbs 24:10 (The Message)). Things will always come to test your resilience so you must be able to bounce back from the setbacks no matter how difficult they may be.

It is at your weakest moment that you know how strong you are. This is where the enemy is expecting you to die, because you have been so battered and bruised and abused. Have you ever seen those boxing matches where the one man is knocked down and he is all weak and bloody? The referee is counting down, 10, 9, 8...2, but just before he gets to 1, when everyone thinks it's over, that man gets up and gets back into the fight.

I decree that you will rise up with more strength and more power to win, even while your enemies are counting down to count you out. When the devil wants you to give up, cave in and quit, begin to dig into the word of God with more fervor and draw strength from His word.

No matter how many times you trip them up, God-loyal people don't stay down long; Soon they're up on their feet, while the wicked end up flat on their faces. (Proverbs 24:16 (The Message)).

Change requires a change in thinking. Be willing to let go of anything that could be a hindrance to you and learn to think differently. Many times we sabotage our progress by how we think. Our thought processes began to take shape early in our childhood, and many of them are subconsciously holding us back. You must be willing to take the time and dig deep to find out what strongholds, soul ties or unhealthy emotional attachments are affecting you. Ask the Holy Spirit to show you any negative thought patterns or belief systems that need to change.

You must be willing to take a stand and separate yourself from people and activities that will hold you back. Make it a point to ignore the negative voices around you. Forgive them for their ignorance of the process that you are going through. Not many people are willing to, or ready for the changes that you may be experiencing, so they will not be able to walk with you. They will not be able to understand what you are going through, and instead of helping, may end up causing hurt and pain. I cannot stress enough how important it is to forgive them. Let nothing of the enemy hinder your elevation process.

During one of these difficult times in my life, two people I loved dearly were celebrating birthdays. Our relationship had become strained and I grappled with the idea of reaching out to them with birthday wishes, wondering how they would take it. I decided to take the high road and sent birthday wishes anyway. They both responded with a simple "Thank you." It was quite different from previous responses, but they responded.

I felt wonderful for having obeyed the leading of the Holy Spirit to reach out to them in spite of the situation. Continuing to show love in these situations can be difficult, but this is where our stretching takes place. No matter how difficult it gets, forgive. Most importantly, keep your eyes on the Lord and choose to praise Him in the face of the devil. Let satan see that nothing will affect your praise and show Him that even in your worst moments, your God remains Supreme.

Can you love through the hurt and the pain? Can you bring yourself to do what is right despite how you feel? Can you maintain your praise when hell is bombarding you? If you can, you are on your way to your next level.

KARLENE MILLWOOD

50.1 Meditation

References: Isaiah 54:1-3a;

1. What stood out for you in this lesson?

2. What are some of the changes you have had to make in your life?

3. What were some of the challenges you faced?

4. What did you do to overcome them?

5. Has your life changed for the better as a result? How?

6. How would you encourage someone else to deal with painful situations?

51 The Law of Love

God's Kingdom is governed by laws and principles.

A LAW is:

1. A principle based on the predictable consequence of an act.
2. The principles and regulations established by some authority and applicable to its people, whether in the form of legislation or of custom and policies recognized and enforced by judicial decision.

A PRINCIPLE is:

1. An accepted or professed rule of action or conduct.
2. A fundamental, primary, or general law or truth from which others are derived.

Love is a principle, so is unity. There is an anointing locked up in unity and can only be unlocked when we operate in the principle of love.

Let's look at the following scriptures to show you how important the principle of unity is:

1. Psalm 133:1 (ERV)
   Oh, how wonderful, how pleasing it is when God's people all come together as one!

2. Matthew 12:25-26 (ERV)
   Jesus knew what the Pharisees were thinking. So he said to them, *"Every kingdom that fights against itself will be destroyed. And every city or family that is divided against itself will not survive. So if satan forces out his own demons, then he is fighting against himself, and his kingdom will not survive."*

3. 1 Corinthians 12:12-14
   The Body of Christ is ONE, albeit with many parts, but the parts function as a cohesive whole.

4. John 17:20-23
   Jesus prayed and asked the Father to make us ONE.

We are different people based on our personalities, but we are ONE in the Spirit based on the character of Christ in us. Love is a fruit of the Spirit and it is Heaven's currency. It is a powerful force that can open or shut doors. When we operate outside of love we shut ourselves off from God, for He is love, and from His benefits. (1 John 4:7-21).

In 2014 while we were rehearsing to do a play that the Lord had given me, I realized that I was getting frustrated a lot with the actors. Some were consistently late, didn't study their lines, or weren't taking what we were doing seriously, in my opinion. All this led to a lack of cohesiveness or ONENESS.

I knew I needed to work on my attitude, so I began to take it to the Lord. I would pray about it before I went to rehearsals and when I got home after rehearsals. Even though each cast member was responsible for their own conduct, as the leader, I was responsible for being an example for them to follow. Therefore my responses had to be grounded in love (patience).

There were many trials and numerous challenges but somehow God got us through it. They gave a stellar performance on opening night. I was very proud of them and the hard work that they put in. At the end of the play, one of the cast members thanked me for my patience with them. Music to my ears. God must have done something in me as a result of those prayers.

When we are ONE we are joined together like the links in a chain. It is difficult for anything to come between us when we are tightly connected. However when one of those links is broken, any little thing can wedge itself in between. Love is the cornerstone of unity. It is only in love that we can be a united force to impact this world for the Kingdom of God. There are many believers but we form one body. *The human body has many parts, but the many parts make up one whole body. So it is with the body of Christ.* (1 Corinthians 12:12 NLT).

We are one in Christ, therefore if I don't love another in the body of Christ, it means I don't love myself. If I hurt another, I am hurting myself. Since we are one with God we are also doing these actions to Him. I have one body and if I hurt any part of my body I feel it throughout my whole being. If I should lose a finger, toe or any other part it would hurt and I would no longer be whole. My body may still function, but with diminished capacity.

So it is in the Body of Christ. When one is hurt we should all feel it. If we lose one, it affects the functioning of the rest of the body. Until we truly come into this understanding we will continue to operate solely as individuals versus a cohesive whole in unity. Love is the foundation for unity in the Body of Christ. *For which of us would willfully mistreat our own body? Do we not love and take tender loving care of it?* (Colossians 1 to 3).

51.1 Meditation

References: Psalm 133:1; Matthew 12:12-14, 25-26; John 17:20-23; |1 John 4:7-21; 1 Corinthians 12:12; Colossians 1 – 3

1. What stood out for you in this lesson?

2. Love is _____.

3. What is the definition of a law?

4. What is the difference between a law and a principle?

5. Why should we strive for unity among believers?

52 Vitamin L

In my quiet time one Sunday morning the Lord said to me, "My people are finding it difficult to love each other because they do not yet understand how much I love them. They don't understand the meaning of my love. They see love separate and apart from who I AM and only as an outward action, a verb, instead of something intrinsic to my nature, and by extension theirs.

So they continue to struggle with receiving My love, with loving themselves and with loving others. For how can love effectively be shown outward when it is not yet manifesting inward? It flows from me first. They don't have to work for my love, it's freely given. Just receive it and accept it and from that knowledge apply it to yourselves. Love you the way I love you. Love Me the way I command you to, and let us form a bond. When that circle is complete, then you will know how to extend it outwards."

God is love, so the only way to defeat divisions and factions in the body of Christ is with God (Love). *And let us consider how we may spur one another on to love and good works.* (Hebrews 10:24 NIV).

God's love has been poured out into our hearts through the Holy Spirit, who has been given to us. (Romans 5:5 NIV).

Deficiencies in our natural bodies often lead to negative manifestations on our skin or in our health. For example, low red blood cells lead to anemia. A lack of vitamins C and D leads to a compromised immune system and so on. Likewise in the body of Christ the same would be true. Divisions, factions, non-constructive criticism, competition, pushing for positions – these are all manifestations of a Vitamin L deficiency.

KARLENE MILLWOOD

I asked the Lord, "But Lord, wouldn't these be more of a lack of knowledge based on faulty teaching from our past?"

"No", the Lord answered. "Knowledge without love is empty; vain."

I thought about this and looked back into the scriptures. I see where we are told to pursue love not knowledge. (1 Cor. 14:1). The Apostle Paul tells us in 1 Corinthians 8:1-3 (NIV), *"we know that we all possess knowledge. Knowledge puffs up, but love builds up. The man who thinks he knows something does not yet know as he ought to know. But the man who loves God is known by God."*

Love is patient – it waits. Love is not self-seeking – it seeks the will of God. *Nobody should seek his own good, but the good of others.* (1 Cor. 10:24 NIV).

As a body, we ought to stop seeing love only as something we talk about, and see it as what we should do and be. God does not only do love. He is love! He is our Father and we are His sons. Therefore we ought to be representing Him. Hebrews chapter 1:3 describes Jesus as the expressed (or exact) representation of the Father's being. We are also to show off His image. He is love, so we should BE love, and from that position of BEING, we will be able to DO; to show that love to others.

The nineteenth century Pentecostal preacher, John G. Lake says, "The secret of Heaven's power is not in the doing, but in the being."

Our primary purpose on earth is to BE sons of God. The secondary purpose is to DO our individual assignments that we were anointed and appointed for before the foundation of the world. (R. Bobby Somers).

The doing gives expression to WHO we ARE; so we have to BE before we can DO. We have to be full of love before we can express it outward genuinely. For that to happen we have to:

- Receive the Father's love and learn to love Him in return – Oneness with God.
- Apply His love internally and learn to love ourselves – Oneness with self.
- Express that love externally to others – Oneness with others.

Our Heavenly Father does not love us because of what we do, but because of who we are; His sons. A love deficiency is really a God deficiency. The absence of love simply indicates the absence of God. Wherever there is negativity, gossip, strife, divisions, God is missing in those lives. Where God is not, there is an opening for satan to work.

Read 1 Corinthians 13 and substitute the word 'God' for every occurrence of the word 'Love'. Gives you a different perspective, doesn't it? As a body we need to get rid of these negative behaviours and "spur one another on to love and good works." Let us love each other as the Lord commands us. Satan doesn't know how to love, but God IS love!

52.1 Meditation

References: Hebrews 10:24; Romans 5:5; 1 Corinthians 10:24; 13; 14:1

1. What stood out for you in this lesson?

2. What is love?

3. What causes strife and divisions in the church? Provide scriptures.

4. What is the secret of Heaven's power?

5. What is the significance of Being and Doing the Kingdom of God?

6. When we operate outside of love who are we pleasing? Why?

7. God is _____.

53 Curses vs. Blessings

According to dictionary.com the word bless means to:

1. Bestow good upon
2. To protect or guard from evil

A blessing is:

1. The invoking of God's favour upon a person
2. Approval or good wishes.

Many years ago when I was a young believer, I met and befriended a young woman. As our friendship grew I came to find out that her living situation was less than ideal. At the time I was living alone in a fairly big house and so I invited her to live with me until she got on her feet. A few months later things started to change. The atmosphere in the house became a little tense as this person started to disrespect me, and my home. Eventually I asked her to leave. It was brought to my attention that she started a smear campaign against me afterwards.

The day when she was moving out of my home she called me a derogatory name and uttered other things which I won't repeat here. When I discussed it with my spiritual mentor at the time, she told me that the young lady cursed me (because of the words she spoke, and words have power).

To curse someone is to:

1. Express a wish that misfortune, evil and doom befall them
2. To invoke evil upon them

The words that the young woman uttered were not nice words and by this definition, she *invoked evil upon me*. My understanding of spiritual things was basic at that point in my walk, so I hadn't yet come to understand how powerful our words are.

My mentor explained to me that I now had to take the word of God and reverse what she spoke over me. Over time I learned how to reverse curses or negative words spoken over me, by appropriating the word of God and speaking it constantly over my life. This experience taught me the importance of studying the scriptures and gaining revelation to apply it to my life daily. Proverbs 4:23 (The Message) teaches us to *keep vigilant watch over your heart, that's where life starts.*

In Luke chapter six, Jesus teaches us about the good tree and the bad tree. He says, *"A tree from good stock doesn't produce scrub fruit nor do trees from poor stock produce choice fruit. 44 A tree is identified by the kind of fruit it produces. Figs never grow on thorns, or grapes on bramble bushes.45 A good man produces good deeds from a good heart. And an evil man produces evil deeds from his hidden wickedness. Whatever is in the heart overflows into speech.* (Luke 6:43-45 TLB).

When our hearts and our thoughts are full of negative things that is what we will speak. When we are full of the word of God that is what we will speak. Renowned Minister and author, Joyce Meyer, tells us in her book, *Battlefield of the Mind*, that we cannot have a positive mind and a negative life or vice-versa. If we want a positive life our thoughts must be positive.

King David asked the question in Psalm 119: 9 (The Message), *"How can a young person live a clean life?"* Then he answers his own question by saying, *"By carefully reading the map of your Word."*

God gave us His word as a map or blueprint to help us live a blessed, stress free and prosperous life in the earth. His word contains everything we need to live a Godly life. When Paul wrote to the Philippians he urged them to, *"fix your thoughts on what is true and good and right. Think about things that are pure and lovely, and dwell on the fine, good things in others. Think about all you can praise God for and be glad about it."* (Philippians 4:8 TLB).

Cindy Trimm told us in one of her blogs that God speaks to us at the *speed of thought.* If you follow Paul's instructions, you will be thinking God-thoughts. God-thoughts are good thoughts because all good things come from above. Anything else is from the evil one. Let us strive to keep our souls pure by feeding it pure thoughts, so that when we speak to, or about, each other our speech will overflow with what is in our hearts; blessings, and not curses.

I've banked your promises in the vault of my heart so I won't sin myself bankrupt. (Psalm 119:11 (The Message)).

53./ Meditation

References: Proverbs 4:23; Luke 6:43-45; Psalm 119:9, 11; Philippians 4:8

1. What stood out for you in this lesson?

2. What does it mean to bless someone?

3. How do you curse someone?

4. Blessings come from _____.

5. Curses are a result of _____.

6. What can you do to ensure you are always speaking blessings over another person?

7. What would you do if someone curses you?

54 Our fortress

A fortress is a fort, stronghold, a place of defense or security, a fortified place[3]. Other sources liken it to a place or source of refuge or support.[4] Numerous scriptures refer to the Lord as our fortress or stronghold. When David was running from Saul, the scripture says he stayed in strongholds in the wilderness. (1 Samuel 23:14).

When David captured Jerusalem from the Jebusites, the scripture says he made the fortress his home (1 Chronicles 11:7). The Psalmist says, *"He only is my rock and my salvation, my stronghold, I shall not be shaken"* (Psalm 62:6 NASB).

The word fortress is derived from the Latin fortis (strong), and facere (to make). When we prophecy that the Lord is our fortress, we acknowledge His strength to protect us, and His ability to make us strong. I got a powerful vision (or dream) of God as our stronghold one morning. I woke up and had my breakfast but I still felt a little tired, so I went back to lay down in my bedroom. I eventually drifted off to sleep and subsequently started dreaming.

I dreamt that I was in my bed in my bedroom and felt the whole room shaking as if it was being rocked by an enormous earthquake. Even my bed was shaking violently. I laid there trying to make sense of it when I saw a man's face come out of nowhere and came very close to mine on the bed. As swiftly as it appeared, it backed up and moved several feet away. As it moved away I saw a wall with some bars at the top rise up in

---

[3] Webster's Unabridged Dictionary
[4] Thefreedictionary.com

KARLENE MILLWOOD

between me and the man. He seemed very upset because he gave me a nasty look just before I woke up.

When I prayed for the understanding and revelation of what I experienced, the Lord revealed to me that I was behind a wall of protection. He literally said the wall was a fortress around me, and its purpose is to keep the enemy out. That man represented the enemy and the wall came up as a barrier between us. The enemy had a plan but he could not touch me because I was shielded in my fortress. It was a very powerful experience and I still think of it in those moments when the devil tries to intimidate and draw me into a place of fear.

I draw upon that image and remind the devil that the Lord did not give me spirit of fear, but of power, love and a sound mind. (2 Timothy 1:7 KJV). When the devil tries to intimidate, attack or distract you, run into the fortress of God's presence and let Him hide you.

I will say of the Lord, He is my refuge and fortress; My God and in whom I trust. (Psalm 91:2 KJV).

54.1 Meditation

References: 1 Samuel 23:14; 1 Chronicles 11:7; Psalm 62:6, 91:2; 2 Timothy 1:7

1. What stood out for you in this lesson?

2. What is a fortress?

3. How is God our fortress?

4. Describe a time when you have experienced God as your fortress.

5. How does the knowledge of God as fortress affect you?

55 Victorious

E ver notice how the enemy always tries to undermine what God is doing in your life? Satan's main goal is for you to become frustrated and start doubting God's activities in and around your life, and lose your faith. Don't believe the lie. No matter what is going on around you, stand firm in your belief that God is a good God. His thoughts toward you are good. (Psalm 139:17 & Jeremiah 29:11). He is interested in you and will always do what is best for you, even if it makes you uncomfortable.

A few years ago, before God took me out of the corporate environment and shifted me into my purpose, I was assigned to a project where satan was trying to do just that. I was blessed to be among several coworkers that were selected to work on a project.

The project manager that I was assigned to was a joy to work with. She was very open and transparent in her interactions with her staff, and we grew to love and respect her for it. She called me aside one day and informed me that another individual had been criticizing me and undermining my credibility and abilities.

Someone else from the team I came from was also complaining and sowing seeds of discord about my involvement with the project. Both of these individuals were trying desperately to get me off that project, and I came under intense scrutiny as a result of these lies. When I heard about it, I felt angry, even though I exercised self-control and kept it contained. There was a particular person that felt intimidated by my abilities and sought to control my every move. But God showed them who was boss, when he shifted me on to that project.

When I went home I took it in prayer to the Lord and He reassured me that I didn't have to worry about them, for where He places me, satan can't shake me. He will definitely try, but God promised that no weapon that is formed against me will prosper. I remember the Holy Spirit showing me a vision of a mouth chattering away the week before. In that moment the Holy Spirit took over and I began to pray in my Heavenly language. When I tried to pray in English, He wouldn't allow me. Little did I know that this is what He was dealing with at that time.

I was led to read Psalm 37:1, *"Fret not thyself because of evildoers, or be not envious of those who do wrong; for like the grass they will soon wither, like green plants they will soon die away.*

In the end God gave me the victory. I continued working on that project until the end of the year. A few weeks after returning to my old department, I was offered a job at another company. I happily resigned from that company and started with a new company several weeks later. The Lord is a protector of those belong to Him. To God be Glory.

But thanks be to God, who always leads us in victory through Christ... (2 Corinthians 2:14a ERV).

55.1 Meditation

References: Psalm 37:1, 139:17; Jeremiah 29:11; 2 Corinthians 2:14

1. What stood out for you in this lesson?

2. What is the devil's main purpose for attacking the believers?

3. How should we respond to his attacks?

4. Why do people fight against each other sometimes?

5. What does the Bible say about people like these?

6. How should we respond to them?

56 Insecurities

T he gifts and talents that God has given me has placed me in the arts and entertainment arena. Not only do I write books, I also write screen and stage plays. As a result I watch a lot of movies and listen to a lot of music. As a child of God, it goes without saying that I am careful about what I set before my eyes as well as the type of music I listen to.

My family and I were watching a movie recently where one of the characters was very wealthy. Although he was wealthy, we noticed that he had an inordinate amount of security guards and pieces of security apparatus in his home. We found it strange that, as wealthy as he is, he still feels insecure and afraid. What would cause someone in his position to feel insecure?

The word insecure speaks of feelings of not measuring up. Insecure people feel insignificant, fearful, unworthy and incapable. What is it that causes these feelings in someone? They often begin in childhood as a result of the environment that they were brought up in. Several factors like parental divorce, a contentious environment, being bullied, or simply being let down by a trusted friend can become the root of insecurity in a person's life.

In her book, So Long Insecurity, Beth Moore talks about satan using doubt as a weapon against believers. She says, "satan loves for us to question who we are and how we measure up to others. He wants us to feel insecure [about] the meaning and purpose of our lives, where we're going and how we'll get there." She continues by saying another source of insecurity is self-reliance. We rely on ourselves too much instead of learning to depend on God.

Insecurities are based in fear, and though it may seem like a conundrum, I dare say there is also an element of pride attached to it. What role could pride possibly play in the life of an insecure person? If insecurity is about not measuring up, then an insecure person is not comfortable revealing their flaws. As a matter of fact they may try to cover them up with a contrived perfection that they find difficult to live up to.

What are some signs of insecurity in a person? Whenever one person tears down another by speaking negatively about them, it is because they are fearful of something about that person. Author and Minister, Cindy Trimm says, "They may fear your intelligence, power or independent thinking. They fear you because they cannot control you and they don't have the capacity for you."

Their insecurities cause them to speak negatively about you, and express frustration toward you. Neither of which are attached to love. The Bible tells us that love is patient (not frustrated), and if we are fearful, love is absent because perfect love casts out all fear. (1 John 4:18 KJV).

An insecure person will try to capitalize on another's admission of ignorance (not having knowledge of a thing). The latter is wise because in admitting to not knowing something, he or she has opened the door to knowledge. The former, locked up in their insecurities and ignorance, gloats at the wise person's admission of not knowing and seeks ways to tear down that person. An insecure person will always want to put you under so that they can feel better about themselves, and they always have to have the upper hand.

But there is good news for you! As a child of God, you don't have to continue to live with insecurity. The scripture says, *"Therefore if any person is [ingrafted] in Christ (the Messiah) he is a new creation (a new creature altogether); the old [previous moral and spiritual condition] has passed away. Behold the fresh and new has come!"* (2 Corinthians 5:17 (The Message)).

No matter the cause of the insecurity, Christ came to set us free, and whom the Son sets free, is indeed free. (John 8:36). I grew up with a lot of insecurities and it took years to be delivered from them. As I write this chapter, I continue to search myself to see if there may be any area where insecurity may still be lurking undetected.

The most effective way to send insecurity packing is to first know who you are, then know who God says you are. Who are you as a unique individual? What does your Heavenly Father say about you? Constant criticism and comparisons to others can make a person insecure. If you don't learn what the word of God says about you, you can become a driveling mess based on people's wrong perceptions of you. I was that way for a long time before my breakthrough came.

It seemed that the most difficult thing for me to break free from, was what people thought about me. It is so dangerous to give attention to people's opinions about you – people who may not even know or understand who you are. I listen to and read inspirations from women like Charis Hillman-Brown, who said, "Those who care less about what other people think and more about what God thinks and what matters most to them, will receive more, because they step out in faith."

That's nice! But how do I get to the point where I care less? It seemed like a daunting, unattainable task. But one day, with the help of the Holy Spirit, I woke up, and for every negative thing that was hurled in my direction, I reminded the devil that, *no weapon turned against [me] will succeed. [I] will silence every voice raised up to accuse [me]. These benefits are enjoyed by the servants of the Lord; their vindication comes from [God]...*" (Isaiah 54:17 NLT).

You have to remember that you are complete in Jesus. You are the apple of his eye, his wonderful inheritance, whose name is tattoed on the palm of His hand. He loves you and He will never leave you nor forsake you. (Colossians 2:10; Psalm 17:8; Isaiah 49:16; Deuteronomy 31:6).

So when those thoughts begin to flood your mind as a result of criticism and negative judgement, fight back with the word of God and let satan know that you know who you are, and whose you are. Kick insecurity to the curb, and know that you are secure in Christ, because all of who He is, is in you.

You are more than a conqueror!

56.1 Meditation

References: 1 John 4:18, 8:36; 2 Corinthians 5:17; Isaiah 54:17; Colossians 2:10; Psalm 17:8; Isaiah 49:16; Deuteronomy 31:6

1. What stood out for you in this lesson?

2. What is insecurity?

3. What are some of the causes of insecurity?

4. Do you struggle with feelings of insecurity? If so, about what?

5. How do you presently handle those feelings?

6. Did this chapter help you in any way?

7. What will you do differently as a result of reading this chapter?

8. What are some other scriptures that can help you to deal with insecurity?

57 Get Drenched

We sometimes pray and ask God for more of Him but one day the Holy Spirit impressed it in my spirit that it is not more of Him that we need. We have all of Him inside us and nothing is lacking. He held nothing back. What we need is to immerse ourselves deeper into Him.

It's like going to the beach. We can put on our bathing suits and stand on, or walk across the sand all day and choose not to go in the water. As long as we are only on the sand, we never get wet. Only when we step off the sand and into the water will we get wet. The further out we go in the water is the more we immerse ourselves in it. If we continue to wade out, we will be eventually covered i.e. fully immersed.

The more we immerse, the more saturated we become and no matter how experienced we may be as swimmers, some water is going to get inside through our mouths, ears or nose. It is hard to immerse yourself in anything without some getting in. What gets in is what will come out. If we immerse ourselves in listening to a certain type of music, we will begin to sing and speak the lyrics that we hear. If we read certain types of books, information from them will be imparted to and flow out of us.

When we have been immersed in water, the first thing we do when we come up is spit [out water]. What goes in must come out. Likewise when we immerse ourselves in Jesus, and the things pertaining to Him, wisdom and knowledge will get inside us and it will come out in our daily conversations and conduct. So it is not more of Jesus that we need. What we need is to immerse, to submerge in Him completely until we are saturated.

Joshua 1:8 TLB says, *constantly remind the people about these laws, and you yourself must think about them every day and every night so that you will be sure to obey all of them. For only then will you succeed.*

The beach is a vast body of water for our use, but we never experience how it feels or tastes until we put ourselves in it. It's the same with Jesus. *Taste and see that the Lord is good. Oh, the joys of those who take refuge in Him.* (Psalm 34:8 NLT).

When a person drowns in natural water they die. Even if they are resuscitated later, they experienced death for a few seconds or minutes. When we drown in spiritual water we become alive. We awaken to new life.

Submerge yourself in Him.

57.1 Meditation

References: Joshua 1:8; Psalm 34:8

1. What stood out in this lesson for you?

2. What is the correlation between water and the Holy Spirit?

3. You step into water to submerge yourself in it. How do you immerse yourself in the Spirit?

4. What are the benefits of immersing in the word of God?

5. List scriptures that speaks of the importance of reading the word of God.

6. How often do you study the word?

58 The Lord's Kingship (Psalm 24)

God as Creator-King

*T*he earth is the Lord's and everything in it. The world and they who
dwell in it. For He has founded it upon the seas and established
it upon the waters. (vv1, 2).

God is the creator of everything and the founder of the earth. Everything
and everyone on earth belong to Him. He owns it all.

For the Lord *is God, and he created the heavens and earth and put
everything in place.*
*He made the world to be lived in, not to be a place of empty chaos. "I am
the* Lord*," he says, "and there is no other.* (Isaiah 45:18 NLT).

The Presence of the King

*Who May Ascend Into The Mountain Of The Lord? Or Who May Stand
In His Holy Place?*

The Holy Place Of The Lord Is His Presence. In The Old Testament, The
Holy Of Holies Was The Inner Sanctuary Of The Temple Where The Ark
Of The Covenant Rested. Only The High Priest Was Able To Enter That
Place And He Could Only Enter After He Had Sanctified Himself.

Jehovah Is The God Of All Gods. Lord Of All Creation And Holiest Of All.
He Is High And Lifted Up. Who, Then, Is Worthy To Stand In His Holy

Presence, Considering Who He Is? Or, Who Can Ever Be Exalted To His Place (Position Of Authority, Throne)?

None Can Ever Be Exalted To His Place. Lucifer Rebelled And Tried To Overthrow God And Was Thrown Out Of Heaven. He Resists The Proud But Gives Grace To The Humble. (Proverbs 3:34; James 4:6; 1 Peter 5:5).

God Continually Invites Us To Come Into His Presence, But There Is A Criteria To Do So.

Those Who Have Clean Hands And A Pure Heart, Who Has Not Lifted Up Himself To Falsehood, Or To Worship Idols, And To Swear Deceitfully (Tell Lies) (V5).

God Is Looking For A People Who Have Purified Themselves By The Washing Of The Word (Ephesians 5:26). Only Those Whose Hands And Hearts Are Pure – *The Lord Desires Purity And Singleness Of Heart* [5]– From Those Who Seek Him.

Like The Priests We Have To Sanctify Ourselves By Living According To The Word Of God In Order For Us To Be Accepted In The Holy Of Holies – His Presence. We Don't Need Priests To Go To God On Our Behalf Anymore, We Have Been Given That Privilege To Approach Him Ourselves Through Christ.

...For You Are A Chosen People. You Are Royal Priests,[G] *A Holy Nation, God's Very Own Possession. (1 Peter 2:9 Nlt).*

We Have Become Kings And Priests In Christ, And Therefore We Go Boldly In His Presence. The Veil Was Torn To Afford Us Free Access To The King. We Are Qualified, Through Christ, To Enter Freely Into God's Holy Presence.

So Let Us Come Boldly To The Throne Of Our Gracious God. There We Will Receive His Mercy, And We Will Find Grace To Help Us When We Need It Most (Hebrews 4:16 Nlt).

This Is The Description Of Those Who Are Allowed To Enter His Presence. This Set Of People Who Draw Near To Him In This Manner Is Guaranteed The Lord's Blessings, Favor, Deliverance And Vindication.

---

[5] Expositor's Bible Dictionary

He Shall Receive Blessings From The Lord And Righteousness From The God Of His Salvation. This Is The Generation Of Those Who Seek Him, That Seek Your Face O God Of Jacob. (V6).

Our Divine Warrior

Lift Up Your Heads O You Gates; Be Lifted Up You Ancient Doors, That The King Of Glory May Come In. (V7).

Some Translations Use Everlasting Doors Or Age-Abiding Doors.

Gates And Doors Represent Barriers Or Safety. You Are Either Inside Or Outside A Gate Or A Door, And Regardless Of Which Side You Find Yourself On, Depending On The Circumstances, It Could Be Something That's Hindering You, Or Keeping You Safe. Three Words Are Used To Describe These Gates And Doors:

1. Everlasting – lasting forever, eternal
2. Abiding – continuing without change, enduring, steadfast
3. Ancient – dating from a remote period, of great age, antique

These ancient doors could also represent old things, old ways of doing things because of old ways of thinking, or generational things, or things from your past that shut out God.

When we lift up our heads – look up to Him as our source of power and open the doors of our hearts to Him, those ancient, everlasting, age-abiding things will move. We will experience deliverance and vindication because of our true, pure worship, and His light will flood our hearts.

Who is this King of Glory? The Lord strong and mighty, the Lord mighty in battle. (v8).

This is speaking of His invincible power. The Lord is strong and mighty – powerful. Psalm 91:1 (AMP) says, *"He who [a]dwells in the secret place of the Most High shall remain stable and fixed under the shadow of the Almighty [Whose power no foe can withstand]*. [Bold mine].

He has never lost a battle and the ultimate battle for dominion has already been won, and can never be reversed. He is invincible!

Lift up your head O you gates; be lifted up you ancient doors, that the King of Glory may come in. Who is this King of Glory? The Lord of Hosts, He is the King of Glory. (v9).

The Lord of Hosts refers to Him as the Commander of the Armies of God. He has hundreds of thousands of battalions of angels under His command. That is why He has never lost a battle. All of the Kingdom of Heaven is behind Him and under His authority. No foe can withstand Him.

Therefore old mindsets, bondages, situations, circumstances, nor all of hell is no match for Him. When He comes in He leads us to His Holy Place where none of these can dwell. Once He comes in they are defeated. He lifts us up to ascend to His Holy mountain. He gives us the victory. He is Lord over everything!

58.1 Meditation

Reference: Psalm 24, 91:1; Isaiah 45:18; Proverbs 3:34; James 4:6; 1 Peter 5:5; Ephesians 5:26; 1 Peter 2:9; Hebrews 4:6

1. What stood out for you in this lesson?

2. Describe God as Creator. Provide other scriptures.

3. Describe God as King. Provide other scriptures.

4. Describe God as warrior.

5. What is the mountain of the Lord?

6. The Lord is described as invincible. What does this mean?

7. What the spiritual significance of gates and doors?

8. What other scriptures talk about gates and doors?

9. Can you find a correlation in the meaning of these scriptures?

10. Why are we guaranteed victory through Christ?

59 Predestination

*E*verything has already been decided. It was known long ago what each person would be. So there is no use arguing with God about your destiny. (Ecclesiastes 6:10 NLT).

Every human being was created with purpose. Each put on earth to carry out a specific assignment. Jeremiah chapter one provides further evidence of this.

I knew you before I formed you in your mother's womb. Before you were born I set you apart and appointed you as my prophet to the nations. (Jeremiah 1:5 NLT).

What did God appoint you as?

In Psalm 139:16 NLT, David reaffirms this by saying, *"You saw me before I was born. Everyday of my life was recorded in your book. Every moment was laid out before a single day had passed."*

Your spirit was created before your body. You existed before you were conceived in your mother's womb. Conception was the beginning of the preparation of your entry into the earth. God was watching over your body as it was being formed in your mother's womb. Your body is not you. You are a spirit. Your body is the house for your spirit, and it allows you to live and function in the three dimensional world. The spirit needs a body to function in this realm. Every spirit was made good for all good things come from above.

KARLENE MILLWOOD

"For I know the plans I have for you," says the Lord. "They are plans for good and not for evil, to give you hope and a bright future." (Jeremiah 29:11 NIV).

God's thoughts towards us are to bring us into the great future He has prepared for us in Christ Jesus. If this is the case, why do so many people fail to fulfill their life's purpose? Also, how is it that unsaved people fulfill their purpose while many who are saved don't? Author James Allen says, "All that a man achieves or fails to achieve, is a direct result of his own thoughts. Our thoughts play a major role in us finding and fulfilling our purpose. We direct our lives with our thoughts.

Satan also uses thoughts, suggestions and imaginations to try to lead us astray. It is in our minds that the battle for our souls take place, therefore we must know how to counter the suggestions and thoughts that satan beams to our minds with the word of God.

We know that in everything God works for the good of those who loved Him. These are the people God chose, because that was His plan. God knew them before He made the world. And He decided that they would be like His Son. Then Jesus would be the firstborn of many brothers and sisters. God planned for them to be like His Son. He chose them and made them right with Him. And after He made them right, He gave them His glory. (Romans 8:28-30 ERV).

If some are predestined to be like Christ, are the rest predestined to go to hell? Jesus said, *"During my time here, I protected them by the power of the name you gave me. I guarded them so that not one was lost, except the one headed for destruction, as the Scriptures foretold."* (John 17:12 NLT).

Yet the scripture also says God does not want any to be lost, or perish, but He wants everyone to repent. (2 Peter 3:9). Is God contradicting Himself? Absolutely not!

Let's examine this. Jesus was crucified before the foundation of the world, which means there had to be a betrayer to hand him over for crucifixion. Judas was not born then, but a spirit was created for which the body of Judas Iscariot was made to live in, in time. In order for the person of Judas Iscariot to become the betrayer, he had to accept the evil (betrayer) spirit. *When Judas had eaten the bread, satan entered into him...* (John 13:27 NLT). This scripture tells us where that spirit originated.

You see that Judas was not predestined to betray Jesus. He accepted the spirit of the betrayer from satan and stepped into that position as the betrayer. Get it? Judas could have chosen to think differently, but instead, he cooperated with satan by accepting the thought satan gave him, and acted on it.

Let's look at this further. Christ is the Spirit. Jesus embodied the Spirit of Christ in the earth. In order for the Spirit of Christ to come into or upon us, we have to accept Christ as Saviour and Lord and step into the position as sons of God.

There are many spirits floating around in the earth. Spirits of infirmity, lust, perversion, rebellion are all evil spirits from the devil. There are also the good spirits of love, meekness, patience, kindness and so on from the Lord. What we embrace determines who we become. Are we going to become who we were predestined to be, or only a shadow of it? Will we go through life without even coming close to discovering who we were meant to be?

Some would argue that Jesus could have chosen a different path. No he could not. Jesus knew the end from the beginning. He knew His assignment (purpose) for coming into the world, so He was able to focus on fulfilling it with the help of the Father. We don't know our purpose from birth, but we discover it as we walk through life. Due to this we are more susceptible to the enemy's traps to derail us, but when we accept the Christ Spirit, He helps us as the Father helped Him.

As long as we are seeking God's Kingdom and moving in purpose, satan will come after us. He tried to stop Jesus, why wouldn't he try to stop us?

Understanding that it's what people choose to accept that determines who they become, then second Peter 3:9 tells me that even those who are being lost have a chance at salvation. If no one accepts the bad (evil) spirits, hell could be empty, but for the lack of knowledge the people are perishing.

Even so God remains patient.

59.1 Meditation

References: 1 John 4:1; Romans 8:28-30; 2 Peter 3:9; john 13:27; Hosea 4:6

1. What stood out for you in this lesson?

2. Explain predestination.

3. What determines who we become?

4. What are we predestined to be?

5. What was Jesus' purpose in life?

6. Could He change it? Explain.

7. Can we change ours? Explain.

8. Why do some people find their purpose while others don't?

60 Seed and Fruit

*B*lessed shall be the fruit of your body and the fruit of your ground. (Deuteronomy 28:4 AMP).

Every tree begins as a seed. Before trees bear fruit they go through a process of growth. And God said, *"Let the earth put forth [tender] vegetation: plants yielding fruit whose seed is in itself, each according to its own kind, upon the earth. And it was so.*

The earth brought forth vegetation: plants yielding seed according to their own kinds and trees bearing fruit in which was their seed, each according to its own kind. And God saw that it was good (suitable, admirable) and He approved it. (Genesis 1:11-12 AMP).

So every tree starts as a seed, grows into a seedling (infant), youth, prime of life, middle age, senior, twilight and then death. [6]The life stages of a tree are much like that of a human. I understand the metaphor that the Psalmist uses in chapter one verse three (KJV), more clearly, when he spoke of the Godly man. *"He shall be like a tree planted by the rivers of water, that brings forth its fruit in its season, whose leaf also shall not wither; And whatever he does shall prosper."*

Just as every tree (or plant) begins with a seed, so does human life. The tree carries its seed in itself as do humans. In order for the tree to reproduce it has to go through the pollination process. Pollination is the sexual reproduction of plants where pollen is transferred from the male part of the plant (gametes) to the female part (carpel).

---

[6] http://arborday.org/trees/lifestages

Human males deposit sperm into the womb of females through sexual intercourse. Therefore all life begins with a seed. Seeds are not only biological in nature, there are also spiritual seeds. The spirit realm is the causal realm; whatever happens in the natural started in the spirit. Before God created anything He thought it out and lived it out in His mind before He spoke it into being. Therefore thoughts are also seeds - spiritual seeds.

In the natural seeds have to be deposited somewhere and influenced by its environs for life to begin. When a seed is planted in fertile soil and left undisturbed, it will grow to maturity. If the soil is not conducive to growth i.e. hard, rocky, polluted, the seed will be stifled and no growth will occur. The same is true in the spiritual realm. The mind is the womb of the spirit and your thoughts are the seeds that you deposit into it. If you put negative thoughts in, then your life will manifest negativity, but if you impregnate your mind with positive thoughts, you will give birth to good things.

What is manifesting in your life? What fruits are growing out of your thought seeds? Is your mind fertile, hard, rocky or polluted soil?

Even so every good tree bears good fruit, but a bad tree bears bad fruit. A good tree cannot bear bad fruit, nor can a bad tree bear good fruit. Every tree that does not bear good fruit is cut down and thrown into the fire. Therefore by their fruits you will know them. (Matthew 7:17-20 NKJV).

Don't be misled--you cannot mock the justice of God. You will always harvest what you plant. (Galatians 6:7 NLT).

Thoughts are the sperm that impregnates the spirit. So when you meditate on God's word you are literally having intercourse with it.

Do not let this book of the Law depart from your mouth; meditate on it day and night, so that you may be careful to do everything written in it. Then you will be prosperous and successful. (Joshua 1:8 NIV).

Jesus answered and said, *"It is written: Man does not live on bread alone, but on every word that comes from the mouth of God.* (Matthew 4:4 NIV).

Your thoughts are powerful. Your words are equally as powerful. Your destiny began in God's thoughts eons ago, before He spoke us into being. That reproductive process is eternal and permeates every living organism today. It is a law that God established before time and put it in the blueprint of creation. Whatever is in the blueprint will come to manifestation if it is followed correctly.

The destiny that God conceived for us so long ago depends on us for fulfillment. God became pregnant with creation and at the appointed time He gave birth to it. That reproductive process continues in all living things. In order to fulfill our destinies we have to do our part. When God made us He gave us the ability to complete what He started. We came equipped with a manual, with lots of instructions, to help us carry out our assignments.

These instructions are written so that if we read them often and meditate on them, we become pregnant with the very essence of God. The Words of the manual become sperm (seed) to our spirits and impregnate us with instructions to do what is necessary to come into and fulfill our purpose and walk out our destiny in the earth.

The scripture says, *"God causes His sun to rise on the evil and the good, and sends rain on the righteous and unrighteous."* (Matthew 5:45b). So even unsaved people who choose to read the Word and put in practice what they read will reap the benefits.

God's word is His law. When a King speaks His word becomes law and those laws govern everyone, including the King. In our society governmental laws work for everyone regardless of nationality, religion or gender. All who live by the law (in obedience to them) get the same results. Those who break the law are outside the law and will reap the consequences of their actions.

I encourage you to learn the laws of the Kingdom of God so that you can please the King and reap the fruit from the good seed you have planted in your life.

60.1 Meditation

References: Deuteronomy 28:14; Genesis 1:11-12; Psalm 1:3; Matthew 4:4, 5:45b, 7:17-20; Joshua 1:8

1. What stood out for you in this lesson?

2. How important are seeds to life? Explain.

3. How are trees similar to humans?

4. What is the relationship between our thoughts and our spirits?

5. How does the spirit realm relate to the natural world?

6. What can you say about the reproductive process after reading this?

61 No Weapon

Weapons have played an important, if sometimes devastating, role in history since the dawn of humanity. They are used for attack or defense in combat, fighting and war. They vary in range, size and capability, so their use is dependent on the circumstance.

Anything can become a weapon when we are faced with a threat. Sticks, stones, cups, plates, even pens and pencils, have all been used at one time or another as defensive tools. The earliest record of an object being used as a weapon is in the book of Genesis when Cain used a stone to kill his brother Abel (Genesis 4). King David also used a stone to slay Goliath (1 Samuel 17).

Weapons have been a common denominator from the very first recorded war in the Bible, when Abram fought the five Kings and reclaimed Lot and his possessions, to the current Islamic Jihadis. As natural wars are real, so are the spiritual wars we fight on a daily basis. The Kingdom of Heaven suffers violence every day, but the Apostle Paul makes us aware that this is not a physical war.

For we do not wrestle against flesh and blood, but against principalities, against powers, against the rulers of the darkness of this age, against spiritual hosts of wickedness in the heavenly places. (Ephesians 6:12).

Our warfare is spiritual. Satan attacks us in the spiritual realm, and his favourite battleground is the mind. Many things that have been attributed to God, does not come from God, but from the devil cleverly disguising himself behind them. For example, sickness and disease are not from God. He is a healer, interested in our holistic health and would never send any attacks against our bodies. By His stripes we were healed. God put health and healing in place for us, so when anything other shows up, it's from satan.

Storms, tsunamis, earthquakes are called 'acts of God' by popular media, but they are wrong. After the flood, God promised Noah that he (God) would never destroy the world with water again. (Isaiah 54:9). God is a God of His word. He is not a man that He should lie.

Look what Jesus did when the storm rose up while He was crossing the river with the disciples. He spoke to the storm and quieted it (Matthew 8; Mark 4). Why would God send something only to turn around and defeat it? Satan will use anything in his arsenal against the world because he knows that there are those who will be quick to blame God for them.

It doesn't matter what the devil comes with though. Jesus promised that the gates of hell cannot prevail against the Kingdom of God. (Matthew 16:18). God also told Israel that many weapons will be formed against them, but none will succeed. He reminded them that He is the One who created the one who made the weapons. Therefore the Greater One is with us and for us.

God gave me a powerful dream early one morning. I dreamt that I was in the yard washing my car. I went to rinse the mats under a standpipe, and as I came up to it, I noticed a minivan filled with men parked nearby. Some of the men had big machine guns pointed directly at me. I put the mats down and walked up to the minivan and ordered them to drop their weapons. I held up what looked like a police badge so they could see it and repeated my instructions. When they saw the badge, they immediately complied.

Then some of them seemed to vanish and now there were only three men in the van. I asked, "Where are the others? Weren't there more of you? Where did they go?"

One of the three stomped his foot on the floor and I noticed the mats on the floor moving. I commanded whoever was underneath to come out. Suddenly the minivan was filled with these men again. They suddenly realized that they far outnumbered me, and picked up their weapons and trained them on me again. I commanded them to lower their weapons or I would call for backup. One of them replied, "It's going to take a while for backup to come, let's finish her!"

Some of my co-workers were standing in the background a little ways from me. I laughed and looked behind me. I raised my voice and shouted, "Backup! I need backup!" Immediately I was surrounded by my co-workers. On seeing this, all but one of the men dropped their guns. This one turned the barrel of his huge submachine gun toward me and pulled the trigger, but nothing happened. I calmly walked over to him and took the gun, by the barrel, out of his hand.

The last image was of my co-workers and I still surrounding these men after having disarmed them. It is a sure reminder that none of the devil's devices will ever work against me or you. We have the authority to disarm him because He is already defeated. We simply have to lift our voices and speak the authoritative word of God, and angels will move on our behalf. We have all of Heaven behind us, so even when we are surrounded and seem to be outnumbered by satan and his demons, we need not panic. There is always more for us, than are against us.

"No weapon that is formed against you will succeed; And every tongue that rises against you in judgment you will condemn." (Isaiah 54:17a NKJV).

61.1 Meditation

References: Genesis 4; 1 Samuel 17; Ephesians 6:12; Isaiah 54:9, 17a; Mark 4; Matthew 8, 16:18

1. What stood out for you in this lesson?

2. What was the first weapon recorded in the Bible?

3. What type of weapons does satan use against believers?

4. What weapons should we counter with?

5. What is God's promise to us as it relates to weapons?

6. Who is responsible for natural disasters?

62 Rightly Handling Failure

E ver failed at something? How did you feel about it? Not too good, right? Trust me, I know the feeling. Your mind is telling you that you should know better. You second guess yourself and ask, why didn't I do this or that differently? Other voices are saying words like stupid, disappointment, not expecting that from you and I could go on and on. Then you begin to feel like you are not good enough. You begin to doubt yourself and start to believe the lie that you can't do anything right.

For years I struggled with overcoming those negative feelings that we attach to failure. I have been thinking about how we handle failure, or making mistakes, a lot lately because of a particular person, who I will call Sandra. Sandra and I were working on a project and she would occasionally forget to do something. When that happened Sandra would apologize profusely, which is good, but what concerned me, was what followed the apology.

Sandra would say things like, "I feel so stupid", "I'm so embarrassed", "I should know better" and so on. Coming from that place myself, I understood what was going on in her mind and tried as best as I could to speak words of encouragement to her. Over time I started to see a change.

There is a popular online game called Candy Crush which taught me something about handling failure the right way. Candy Crush challenges you mentally to complete the different levels and keep advancing to higher levels. With each level it becomes more challenging. When I complete a level successfully, a little cartoon girl claps her hands and jumps jubilantly, cheering me on. However, if the level was too challenging and I was not able to complete it successfully, the same little girl stands there looking dejected with the message, "You have failed to complete this level."

I used to play the game often because it is one of those that you can become easily addicted to. What caught my attention and made me think was this: each time I 'fail' a level, I am eager to press the retry button and go at it again without even thinking twice about it. I just do it because now it has become a challenge that I have to overcome. Besides I am anxious to see what the next level holds. Hmmm. Interesting.

This got me thinking about life. Each level of Candy Crush is a test of my mental agility. I have to pass the test to move to the next level. As it is in the game, so it is in life. In school we are tested to advance to higher grades. When we do well on the job, we are promoted. God also builds tests into life to help us to advance to higher levels. Many times we fail those tests because we are looking at them from the wrong perspective. But He is a God of second chances and He will allow us to go through the test again and again until we can pass it and move forward.

Sometimes you feel that for every two steps you take forward, you take four steps back. Be encouraged. It takes faith to get up and try again. The Apostle Paul describes faith as a race, but this race is not a sprint. It's a marathon. It's long distance running. You have to give yourself permission to fail, but when you do, don't stay there.

Every failure is meant to teach you something about yourself. Submit the failures to God and He will turn it around for your good and His glory. Most importantly, take the lessons from the failures and apply them to your situations to help you move forward. Proverbs chapter twenty four verse sixteen in the New Living Translation says, *the godly man may trip seven times, but they will get back up. But one disaster is enough to overthrow the wicked.*

No matter how many mistakes you have made, or how many times you have failed, get back up. Get up! Keep on going! Leave the negative thoughts of failure behind you and look ahead. The Apostle Paul said it like this:

...I focus on this one thing: Forgetting the past and looking forward to what lies ahead, I press on to reach the end of the race and receive the Heavenly prize for which God, through Christ Jesus, is calling us. (Philippians 3:13b-14 NLT).

You have to forget in order to advance. Make a conscious decision to leave negative thoughts of failure behind. Repent where necessary and forgive yourself. Learn from the mistakes then boldly keep moving forward.

62.1 Meditation

References: Proverbs 4:16; Philippians 3:13b-14

1. What stood out for you in this lesson?

2. Why are we afraid of failure?

3. How do you handle your failures?

4. How will that change after reading this chapter?

5. What do you think is the right way to handle failures?

6. What is the benefit of a failure?

63 Creation

Before anything else existed, God's Kingdom did. Genesis 1:1 (KJV) says, *"In the beginning God created the Heavens (plural) and the earth.* (Parenthesis mine).

I believe that *beginning* was long before His Spirit moved and started to re-create or reform in Genesis 1:3. What God was doing was re-establishing order to what He already created. Let's be clear. The scripture does not explicitly say this, however it's something that was imparted to my spirit as I meditated the first book of Genesis a few years ago.

In the very beginning God established His everlasting Kingdom, which consists of Himself, His Son and the Holy Spirit in the Triune Godhead as Supreme ruler. The angels were created to serve – every Kingdom has servants. The planets, including earth, were created. Of all the planets only earth had life on it. Here, I offer the theory that it was during this time that dinosaurs and other pre-historic animals existed. Notice the word pre-historic.

The prefix 'pre' means before, therefore, pre-historic suggests that something pre-dates time. They existed before history. During this pre-historic time period everything was beautiful and perfect, because God makes all things perfect. There was no need for natural light because everything was lit by the Presence (Spirit of God), but something happened between verses one and two to change things. What happened to make the earth empty and dark?

Now the earth was formless and empty, and darkness was over the surface of the deep, and the Spirit of God was hovering over the waters. (Genesis 1:2 NIV).

Scientists have long said that a cataclysmic event happened to cause extinction of dinosaurs and other sea creatures millions of years ago. Some believe it was a meteor, others believe it was flood of mass proportions, like the one for which Noah built the ark. Yet, no one has come up with a definitive cause for the extinction.

It is plausible that this period ended by a meteor and a flood. In Luke 10:18 (NKJV) when Jesus was speaking to His disciples who were excited that demons submitted to them in His Name, He told them, "I saw satan fall like lightning from Heaven." Satan was cast out of Heaven because pride filled his heart and he wanted to overthrow God. Other recorded accounts of this can be found in Isaiah 14:12-15 and Ezekiel 28:12-18.

A meteor is defined as a shooting star or falling star. Asteroids are even bigger than meteors, however I allude to falling star because of how satan is described in Isaiah fourteen. In the New International Version he is called morning star. The Amplified Bible describes him as light-bringer and daystar. He was a being of light.

When a star falls out of the sky it has an impact on the earth's atmosphere. Some minor, some major. Imagine an angelic, celestial being of light falling out of Heaven to the earth. The fall of satan and one third of the angels would have an impact on the earth's atmosphere. This was no ordinary little fall. They were thrown out violently. Imagine these strong, powerful beings warring against each other. One angel can destroy one hundred and eighty-five thousand men (2 Kings 19:35), so imagine their size and power.

Now imagine one of them falling out of the sky without restraint and landing on earth. Then imagine hundreds of thousands of them falling to earth. That is a catastrophic event and I dare to suggest that is what happened to cause the imbalance in earth's atmosphere. Whenever sin touches something, it changes it for the worse.

The expulsion of these fallen beings upset the delicate balance that was set by God and caused mass flooding leading to the death of most life forms during that time period. It created a terrible darkness over the earth. These former beings of light were no longer living in the Presence of Light

(God's Presence), and so were no longer reflecting His light. They became darkened and the environment reflected their darkness.

We know that the spiritual realm is the causal realm, therefore what is happening in the spirit will manifest in the natural. Sin tainted what was beautiful and full of life and caused it to become ugly and lifeless. The presence of satan and his demons created chaos in the atmosphere and interrupted the perfect balance of life that God originally created. So in verse three of Genesis one, God's Spirit came back to correct the devastation and restore the earth's original splendor. Then He continued what He began and completed it on the 7th day.

It took me a long time to accept that this revelation came from the Holy Spirit. I struggled with it for a long time because I had never heard anyone else say it before. But God is faithful and led me to find a teaching from a man named Charles Capps, who taught the very same thing that I wrote above. I was blown away and thanked God for the confirmation.

If you get a chance find his teaching on Angels on YouTube and listen, then pray and ask the Lord to give you a revelation of this. This is definitely food for thought, so think on these things.

63.1 Meditation

Reference: Genesis 1; Isaiah 14:12-15; Ezekiel 28:12-18; Luke 10:18

1. What stood out for you in this lesson?

2. What are your thoughts on the creation story in Genesis?

3. How does the scripture describe satan before his fall?

4. How many angels were cast out of Heaven with satan?

5. What was the sin or sins that caused them to be thrown out?

6. How has their presence affected Earth's atmosphere?

64 Just Stop

Every so often situations come to challenge my identity and lead me to think about my self-worth. Who am I? Am I valuable? Nowadays when it happens it leads me to greater revelation of who I am in Christ. I was meditating on this again recently when this thought came to me:

You have to know your worth, because if you don't, someone else will put a price tag (value) on you and it won't be the full price. Selah.

I read over some notes that I had made on this subject in times past and this one stood out to me:

Our superiority (value) comes from this simple truth: Greater is He that is in me, than He that is in the world,..."

When you know whose you are, and Who resides in you, then you know that you are empowered to overcome any negative situation that presents itself.

I can do all things through Christ who strengthens me. (Philippians 4:13 KJV).

I understand that in order for this to become my reality, all that I am and everything I do, must be submitted to Christ. I live from Him being my source in every way, *for in Him we live and move and exist, for we are His children.* (Acts 17:28). So many people are still looking for value in the things that they do. They push to do things that will get them noticed because people's praise is important to them. It is important to them to be seen by others and if not, they feel less-than (devalued).

When we seek to find our personal value in things or in other people, we make them our god. We worship these things and people as if we fail to exist without them. I see this a lot in the creative and performing arts. Many who sing, act, dance, paint etc. begin to pay an inordinate amount of attention to the gifts instead of the Giver of the gifts. They set up the gifts as idols in their lives, instead of submitting them to the Giver to use them for His purpose.

Every word of scripture is important, however this verse is key to understanding how we should operate in the Kingdom of God:

Seek the Kingdom of God above all else, and live righteously, and He will give you everything you need. (Matthew 6:33 NLT).

Everyone wants the things, but are unconcerned about the seeking. We want the blessings but we don't want to wait. We want the glory but we don't want the process. Personally, in the early part of my process, I hated it. For a great deal of that time I felt angry, frustrated and went through much of it with a spirit of grief. I kept looking at it as something negative and missed the blessings as a result.

Paul teaches us that *godly grief produces a repentance that leads to salvation without regret, whereas worldly grief produces death.* (2 Corinthians 7:10 ESV).

My mind had to be transformed in this area for me to realize what God was doing in my life, walk it out in victory and get my blessings. The story of Job played a major part in helping me to change my thinking. Job said, *"Though he slay me, yet will I trust in Him. I know my Redeemer lives"* (Job 13:15, 19:25 KJV).

I watch so many people struggle to do what they want, instead of seeking the Lord's will. Lord knows I used to be guilty of that, until understanding got a hold of me and I learned how to rest in God. I learned how to give everything – surrender it all – to God, and trust Him to tell me what to do. That was the moment when my struggling ceased. Only those who believe (in faith) will enter His rest (Hebrews 3:10-11).

I remember someone crying to me, "I don't want to be an Evangelist or a Pastor or a... I just want what is mine." Yet this person was not willing to surrender all, pick up their cross and follow Him.

Well…hello…what if what is yours is to be an Evangelist, or a Pastor? You would be rejecting what is yours because you are not willing to stop, seek and listen. The things you are rejecting, may be the very things that were ordained for you, but you will never know until you just stop. Shhh.

You cannot come into what you reject. And what happened to His will and not mine? Thy Kingdom come, thy will be done on earth as it is in Heaven. Instead of reciting it like a poem, stop and ask God to give you a revelation of this verse. Solomon says, *"you make many plans, but the Lord's purpose will prevail."* (Proverbs 19:21 NLT).

First John 2:15-17 NLT warns us not to love the world or the things of the world. *The world offers only cravings for physical pleasure, pride in our achievement and possessions but they are not from the Father. These are all fading away but whoever does what pleases God, lives forever.*

Do you want the best of what God has for you? Then stop. Just stop. Seek. Listen.

Selah.

64.1 Meditation

References: Philippians 4:13; Acts 17:28; Matthew 6:33; Job 13:15, 19:25; Hebrews 3:10-11; Proverbs 19:21; 1 John 2:15-17

1. What stood out for you in this lesson?

2. What gives you value?

3. What verse of scripture tells us how should we live in the Kingdom of God?

4. How important is it to seek the will of God, and why?

5. How can someone reject what God wants to do in his or her life?

6. What are three things John tells us not to love?

65 Quality of Life

Q uality of life is defined as, the standard of health, comfort and happiness, experienced by an individual or group. Psychologists and business pundits have designed different theories that captures the essence of what determines quality of life for humanity. One of these is called the Pyramid of Mastery, used by certain motivational speakers to depict the most important facets of life that contribute to quality of life. It includes the following (ascending):

i. The physical body
ii. Emotions and meaning
iii. Relationships
iv. Time
v. Career and mission
vi. Finances
vii. Contribution and spirituality

It is suggested that we have to master these seven areas of life in order to live an extraordinary life.

Another well-known tool used in this discussion is Maslow's Hierarchy of Needs, which is thought to motivate human behavior. These needs are (ascending):

i. Physiological: which includes, food, water, sex, sleep etc.
ii. Safety: security of self, employment, good health, property
iii. Love/Belonging: friendship, family, sexual relations
iv. Esteem: self-esteem, confidence, achievements, respect
v. Self-actualization: morality, creativity, problem-solving etc.

When the basic needs are met, self-actualization occurs and the person is ready to live their best life. While we are on the quest of self-actualization, humanity often falls into problems because we try to do things on our own, instead of trusting God to be our Source, and do what He said He will do.

A child of God never has to worry about their needs being met. The scripture tells us that God knows our needs before they arise, and He will supply all of them according to His riches in glory in Christ Jesus (Matthew 6:8; Luke 12:22-34; Philippians 4:19). Therefore, as we grow in knowledge of God's promises, and begin to apply them to our lives, we will come to a place where we are living our best lives every day.

Both of these insightful theories focus on quality of life now, while we are living. However something happened a while ago that made me realize that, while quality of life is important now, it also has eternal consequences.

There is a sister I know that sends out a scripture by text every morning. One morning the verse she sent was taken from Proverbs 15:11. In the New Living Translation (NLT) it reads, *"Even death and destruction hold no secrets from the Lord. How much more does He know the human heart?"*

The same verse in the New Century Version (NCV) reads, *"The Lord knows what is happening in the world of the dead, so He surely knows the thoughts of the living."*

The second translation turned on a light in me and I began to think about life after death. I had not given it much thought before but this translation brought it to me in such a tangible and profound way. When we die – our physical bodies expire – each spirit/soul goes to either Heaven or hell, and God knows where each one is, and what they are doing. How much more we who are living (still alive) in the natural, physical world.

The spirit world is more real than this three dimensional world. When our bodies die we go to another phase of our existence: back to the spirit stage, which is what we truly are; spirit. Our loved ones who have died are *living* either in eternal bliss or eternal torment, but they are still existing in another realm.

As I thought about it, it became clear to me that quality of life goes beyond present, physical needs to the more important thing which is the quality of life of the spirit-man, the most important part of us. The apostle Paul counsels his protégé, Timothy, about this by saying, *"Physical training is good, but training for godliness is much better, promising benefits in this life and in the life to come."* (1 Timothy 4:8 NLT).

This really brings the question of what happens after death into fuller focus for me. How I live my life in the natural determines how I will live in the next phase after my body expires. If I live to please God (attaining true spirituality), I will live with Him in paradise forever. If not, then I will exist in eternal torment, even if I achieved self-actualization by living a quality life now.

The moral of the story is simply this:

Quality of life in LIFE, determines quality of life after death.

How will you spend your eternity?

65.1 Meditation

References: Proverbs 15:11; 1 Timothy 4:8

1. What stood out for you in this lesson?

2. What does quality of life mean to you?

3. Based on the information provided above, how would you describe your quality of life?

4. What are some of our basic needs, and what does the scripture say about them?

5. What plans did God put in place to ensure we will have quality of life on Earth?

6. What is the correlation between quality of life now and in the hereafter? Provide scriptures.

66 Answered Prayers

D on't you just love it when you get a direct answer to your prayers? I know I do. It is such a boost to my faith. It gives me confidence to keep on going to my Father with my requests. He tells us, *"Don't worry about anything; instead, pray about everything; tell God your needs, and don't forget to thank Him for His answers."* (Philippians 4:6 TLB).

Isn't it awesome that you have a confidante whom you can share everything with? Someone you can trust with your information, knowing that no matter what, He is only thinking the best for and about you?

I don't know what I would do without God in my life. Seriously. Friends or family may call you needy or clingy if you call to talk to them about things on a regular basis, but God will never call you such ugly names. You are the sheep of his pasture. He is your Shepherd who leads you into right paths for His name's sake. (Psalm 23).

He will always lead you to go the right way because His reputation is on the line. Revelations like this makes me excited. God will not do anything to sully His reputation, therefore as long as I allow myself to be led by Him, I will do honour to His reputation, and that is what I desire. The Psalmist gives us this command: *Take delight in the Lord, and He will give you your heart's desires.* (Psalm 37:4 NLT).

All these reassurances make it easy for me to go to Him with every little thing. I remember when I did my first stage play a few years ago. To be honest the turnout and response to it went beyond my imaginations. To God be the glory.

There came a time when I wanted to do it again. Some of the crew members and I met with someone who was interested in having the play done at their location. It was a very good discussion but at some point in the conversation I started to wonder if I should do it again. There were so many trials and situations that we had to deal with leading up to opening night that it left us feeling depleted. And truth to be told, some were still getting over hurtful situations and personal difficulties that popped up during that time.

When the meeting ended and I got in my car I prayed about it and asked God for direction. I told Him, "I just need a word from you to let me know if it is in your will for me to do this play again."

He is a faithful God. By the next morning I had my answer through a scripture that someone sent to me. *But you should be strong. Don't give up because you will get a reward for your good work.* (2 Chronicles 15:7). Very direct huh?

To top it off I had also asked Him about a personal situation that I was dealing with. I asked Him how He wanted me to handle the situation. My answer for this came in one of the daily devotionals that I read. The author of the devotional talked at length about ignoring distractions and staying focused on what God called us to do.

As soon as I read it I knew it was my answer. The Blog spoke about ignoring the petty little things that annoy us and drew the analogy of flies in the house. Moments later I got a random text from a friend saying [paraphrase]:

We must not let anything take our focus off our goal, which is Christ. With the single-mindedness of an athlete in training, we must set aside the things that weigh us down and forsake those things that may distract us from being effective in serving Christ.

Both these prayers were prayed the same night and both answers came the next day. How's that for answers? I have so many other testimonies of receiving answers to my prayers that it would take another book to mention all of them. I encourage you today to bring all your cares and worries to the Lord. He is able to do abundantly, exceedingly more than you can ask or imagine according to the power that is working within you. (Ephesians 3:20).

Exercise your faith and pray without ceasing.

KARLENE MILLWOOD

66.1 Meditation

References: Philippians 4:6; Psalm 23, 37:4; 2 Chronicles 15:7; Ephesians 3:20

1. What stood out for you in this lesson?

2. What is the purpose of prayer?

3. Why does God answer our prayers?

4. Why is it important to pray without ceasing?

5. If you were to share some times when God answered your prayers, what would they be?

6. List some scriptures where God guarantees an answer to our prayers.

67 The Goodness of God

In scriptures God is referred to as:

- Supreme
- Sovereign
- Miraculous
- Creator
- Powerful or Strong
- Deliverer
- Waymaker
- Protector
- Defender
- Leader or Guide
- Provider
- Good

He is described by many other attributes, but for this lesson we will focus on Him being good, or, His goodness. God's goodness flows out of His love, and His love flows out of His goodness. His mercy flows out of His love and so does His kindness. They are not separate. God doesn't just do good, or show mercy or have love. He is all of these. Everything about God is good and Psalm 92:5 says there is no evil in Him. Scriptures abound with messages about the goodness of God (See meditation).

God is a good father who desires only the best for His children. Just as our earthly parents do good things for us, and want the best for us, so God desires to see us prosperous. Prosperity is not referring to the erroneous striving for money and things that the world focuses on.

Godly prosperity begins in the spirit, affects the soul and is lived out daily. *Beloved, I pray that you may prosper in every way and [that your body] may keep well, even as [I know] your soul keeps well and prospers.* (3 John 1:2 AMP). When our spirits and souls are prosperous, the rest of our lives will be prosperous.

In order to receive all that God desires to be to us and give us, we must be absolutely sure that He is good. Later in the chapter, John counsels Gaius to imitate what is good. He says, *"Beloved, do not imitate evil, but imitate good. He who does good is of God; he who does evil has not seen (discerned or experienced) God [has enjoyed no vision of Him and does not know Him at all].* (3 John 1:11 AMP).

When we imitate what is good, we are imitating God, because all good things come from Him. He does not cause sickness and disease, nor calamities and disasters. He came to give us life more abundantly. Our good God always gives more…abundantly, exceedingly more.

This is how God loved the world: He gave His Son, His one and only Son. And this is why: so that no one need be destroyed; by believing in Him, anyone can have a whole and lasting life. (John 3:16 (The Message)).

He gave us the best of Himself because He has our best interests at heart. The Psalmist reflects on God's goodness this way:

How precious are your thoughts toward me O God. How great is the sum of them. If I should count them, they would be more than the sand; when I awake, I am still with you. (Psalm 139:17-18 NLT).

As women we fill many roles in society. We are mothers, daughters, teachers, executives, wives, single, and so on. Many of us wear several hats and there are times when life's pressures take a toll. If you find yourself in a situation where it seems like, or feels like, your world is caving in and there is no one there to help, remember that you have a good God who is your everlasting help. He is just waiting for you to call on Him. Go ahead. Call out to Him. Throw all your cares and burdens at Him. He can handle them.

King David was confident in God as his helper when he wrote, *"I look up to the mountains – does my help come from there? My help comes from the Lord, who made Heaven and Earth.* (Psalm 121:1-2 NLT). One day David saw some people going up into the mountains to worship. They must have seemed quite a sight to cause David to stop and reflect and pen these verses.

David knew that the mountain could not help Him. There was a Greater One than the mountain; the One who created the mountain. With this revelation, he proclaimed, *"My help comes from the Lord, who made Heaven and Earth."*

Declare that over your situation today and release the goodness of God to take control. Remember He is your present help in time of need (Psalm 46:1). He is good and He is merciful.

Put your trust in Him and experience His goodness today.

67.1 Meditation

Reference: Psalm 34:8; 46:1, 92:5; 136; 139:17-18, 121:1-2, 145:7; Matthew 19:17; Mark 10:18; Luke 18:19; James 1:17; 3 John 1:2, 11; John 3:16

1. What stood out for you in this lesson?

2. What are some of the ways in which God has been good to you?

3. What does God's goodness entail?

4. When we imitate good, we are imitating _____.

5. When we imitate evil, we are imitating _____.

6. How is God's goodness revealed in scriptures?

7. What kind of thoughts does God think about us? Provide scriptures.

68 Growing Up

rowth is tiring and painful. It's like being pregnant. When the pregnancy is young the mother may feel fine, but as the baby grows inside her she begins to experience discomfort as her body is being pushed and stretched every which way. It becomes difficult to walk, sit or get up. She may even feel some pain doing these things. When it is time to give birth there is a breaking of her water, and then comes the real pain as she pushes to give birth.

It's the same thing when we are growing. There are feelings of discomfort, anxiety, uncertainty and pain. The pain usually shows up in the form of a betrayal, loss of a loved one, or the removal of something familiar. You feel like you are out of your element but you have to push through it with prayer.

Dianna Hobbs in her Empowering Everyday Women Devotional said, "Often our greatest hurts pave the way to reap our greatest harvests. What seems like major detours set us on the right path to fulfill God's dreams for us."

Many times we view adversity as a setback. Something meant to push us backwards instead of forward. With this mindset we could easily miss what God has planned for us. That is why it is important to stay in the Presence of the Lord and ask Him to show you what to do during these times.

As you devote yourself to prayer and seeking God through these difficult times, He begins to reveal things to you, direct you to where He wants you to go, and to do what He wants you to do. You will notice some major changes happening in your life, including some of your relationships. Friends who used to be there before are no longer there. People begin to seem different than what you thought they were. In other words they start to show their true colours.

Understand that God prunes your life through adversity. His purpose for doing that is so that you will grow in wisdom and become stronger to stand surefooted at your next level. He wants you to burst forth and bear much fruit. Adversity is a universal law that is designed for our growth and advancement. This is something that I had to learn, and hopefully after reading this, you will also begin to think of it that way.

In order to move forward to your next level, you will have to shed some things. These things include people, habits and possessions. You may even have to move to a new place, leaving all that is familiar behind. Hebrews chapter twelve verses one and two encourages us to strip off (lay aside) anything that slows us down or holds us back, and keep our eyes on Jesus who is the author and finisher of our faith.

Someone referred to this as the Place of Nothingness. It's a place where you have come to the end of yourself - your natural abilities, and depend on God's abilities to see you through and get you over.

When God was shifting me into my next level, I persisted in prayer. God spoke to me continuously during this time, telling me what to do at each step. When He told me to leave my home and move to the West Coast, I thought for sure I heard wrong. I prayed for confirmation and when the confirmation came, I prayed for confirmation of the confirmation. I asked the Lord to send someone who didn't know about any of what I was going through to tell me what He wants. That very day someone who was visiting from another country came to my home with a friend.

As we fellowshipped and prayed together the Holy Spirit began to speak, and the visitor said the Lord said to tell you yes. I knew it was the answer to what I had prayed that morning and I gave God thanks. We all worshipped Him for His sovereignty. I came to a place of acceptance after that.

Don't fret. He is a restorer. Whatever you willingly give up for Him, He will restore to you. Just ask Job. Job went through his own valley of despair but in the end the Lord restored to him twice what he lost. (Job 42:10)

It was in my place of nothingness that I began to write. It started off with poetry, then I wrote a book that I had been dreaming about since I was a teenager. From that it grew into writing plays and movies, and now this book.

Had I not gone through these harrowing experiences, I would not have discovered my gift nor how God wants me to use it to bring Him glory. We cannot escape the growth experience. God deliberately established it as a law for our benefit, to take us to new heights with and in Him. The next time adversity comes, don't panic. Just use it to grow and rise to your next level.

68.1 Meditation

References: Hebrews 12:1-2; Job 42:10

1. What stood out for you in this lesson?

2. What is adversity?

3. What are some of the signs that you are growing or shifting?

4. What is the Place of Nothingness?

5. True or False - adversity sets us back. Explain your answer.

6. If handled correctly, how can adversity help us?

69 The Big Bang

In my meditation one morning I thought about our existence on earth. I thought about how humanity was created by a loving God, who is our Father, and given this planet to rule, but still not many in the world know that. They do not realize that they exist because GOD IS. He is the Source of all life. If He ceases to exist, everything else ceases to be. The entire universe was created out of His love, and He specifically created Earth for his offspring.

His intent was to reproduce Himself through humanity and produce Godkins (or the God kind). Adam was a perfect being, taken out of the Supreme Being, and with Eve they would give birth to others like themselves and populate the planet. Humanity was created to live and operate forever like God, even continuing the law of creation and expanding it to other planets and galaxies.

God placed that desire in the DNA of humanity, that is why NASA scientists are doggedly looking for life on other planets. Lately the preoccupation with finding life on Mars, or living in space, has taken on a twist, with companies offering space vacations. Although this may seem strange to some, it is quite normal. These scientists are doing what was deposited in their DNA when God put Adam on Earth. The quest to go to other planets and galaxies is a normal thing for humanity, because we are wired for it as a part of God's divine plan. However what should have been easy for Godkins, is now proving difficult for fallen man.

In their flawless state, man may have been able to travel to distant planets at the speed of thought, but because sin entered, we now have to build vessels to take us there. Sin devalued and weakened humanity to the point where we have forgotten our origin and identity, and refuse to acknowledge the source of our existence.

As I meditated that morning, I saw an image of God ceasing to be. Immediately everything else disappeared. They didn't stop or freeze in position, they vanished and there was nothing. What does nothing look like? I could not describe it because there weren't any languages. All language had also disappeared. Can you imagine nothing?

Will humanity ever recognize God as the Source of all life? Scientists continually talk about the Big Bang Theory. I am glad it is referred to as a theory, because that is what it is. However, let's say a BANG occurred. It could not have happened without God speaking. Until He said, "Let there be...", there could be no bang, and when He did speak, I dare say the result was a BOOM instead of a BANG.

If only these intellectual types would go one step backward they would encounter life's true Source, and no longer waste hours disputing useless theories. They spend so much time focusing on what is happening in the world, trying to find their own answers, instead of consulting the Source of all wisdom.

The Lord is the Source of wisdom; knowledge and understanding come from his mouth. (Proverbs 2:6 ERV).

If they would take a step back, they would see a bigger picture and come in contact with the One who has all the answers. Without the I AM everything we hold dear ceases to be, and there would be no big bang to discuss or theorize. The scriptures abound with information that scientists continue to search for.

The Lord by skillful and godly Wisdom has founded the earth; by understanding He has established the heavens. By his knowledge the deeps were broken up, and the skies distill the dew. (Proverbs 3:19-20 AMP).

In the midst of his suffering, Job and his friends had a lot to say about his condition. In chapter thirty eight God had had enough of their debates and He began to challenge Job by asking him some questions:

Where were you when I laid the foundations of the earth? Tell me if you know so much. Who determined its dimensions and stretched out the surveying line? Who supports its foundations; and who laid its cornerstone as the morning stars sang together and all the angels shouted for joy?

Have you ever commanded the morning to appear and caused the dawn to rise in the East? Have you made the daylight spread to the ends of the earth, to bring an end to the night's wickedness? (Job 38:4-7, 12-13 NLT).

God's original plan was flawless. He wanted to colonize Earth with the culture of Heaven, but sin entered, God's perfect design for humanity became corrupted, and the plan was interrupted. When Adam and Eve sinned they began to produce after their own (now flawed) kind – imperfect beings tainted by sin. When sin entered it brought spiritual and natural death, and humanity's lifespan began to decrease.

Jesus Christ came to bring us redemption, so those of us who have accepted Him as Lord and Savior reclaimed our former spiritual state and have once again become immortal spirits. When our natural bodies expire in this phase of life, we will actualize with God in the spiritual realm from where we originated.

Thankfully not all scientists are interested in disproving the existence of God. In the documentary *God of Wonders* (available on YouTube), a group of believing scientists uses the Bible to prove that God also created science. They showed us that science proves the existence of God, and scripture agrees with many scientific discoveries of our time. I encourage you to take the time to watch it as a companion to this lesson.

God is the Source of all life, and He spoke the Big Bang into being.

KARLENE MILLWOOD

69.1 Meditation

References: Proverbs 2:6, 3:19-20; Job 38:4-7, 12-13

1. What stood out for you in this lesson?

2. What is the Big Bang Theory?

3. What caused the big bang?

4. How does it relate to the creation story in Genesis?

5. What proof do we have that God is the source of all life?

6. What was God's original plan for humanity?

7. Where does humanity stand in relation to that plan today?

70 Honor the Father

I have written elsewhere in this book about my love for the little ones. I love children and there are those who love me just as much. To God be the glory!

They brighten my day with their cute little personalities and their laughter. My heart is overjoyed when I have children around me. They often make me think about the love of my Heavenly Father. There are some very special children in my life. One of the things I really enjoy about them is how they rush to throw their arms around me when I walk into a room, or meet them somewhere.

They do this without inhibition and with complete trust. Then when we are settled they talk to me about what is happening in their lives. It's the things that are most important to them, maybe it's just how their day went, or something that happened at school or home, or they may be following up to remind me of a promise I made to them.

These children love me because I have proven to them that I love them, and that they can trust me. How have I done this? By:

- Telling them I love them every chance I get
- Acknowledging their uniqueness and telling them how special they are
- Listening to what they have to say
- Watching out for their safety
- Doing special activities with them
- And so on…

All of these things demonstrate my love for them.

So it is with our Heavenly Father. We love Him because He loved us first. I have done a few things for these children at regular intervals, but our Heavenly Father daily loads us with benefits. (Psalm 69:19 KJV).

Think about it. If a child can love me this much for doing a few things, how much more should we love our Father who bears our burdens day by day? I spent some time studying this verse and this is what I found.

Benefits: (n) Something that is advantageous or good. For example, a payment or gift made to help someone.

Daily: (adj) Computed or measured by the day, e.g. daily quota, a daily wage.

Loadeth: (n) Anything put in or on something for conveyance or transportation, e.g. freight, cargo.

The quantity can be or usually is carried at one time, as in a cart, carload, wagon load.

Putting the meanings of these words together, what we have is a Father who puts on us for conveyance or transportation, a daily quota of gifts or things that are advantageous, or good for us to help us. Bear in mind that gifts are not necessarily referring to material things, but also and more importantly spiritual things. He exchanges our heavy burdens with his light ones.

I am not the natural parent of the children that I am using as reference in this meditation, but I give them what could be considered good gifts. I give them of myself. I give them time. I listen to them and so on. I am sure their own parents do better than me and give more than I give. Yet what we receive from our Heavenly Father outweighs it all.

When a parent, or other adult, treats a child well, that child will automatically want to do things to please that person. Most children know that good behavior gets rewarded. It is no different with us and our Heavenly Father. When we walk in His will for our lives, we see the manifestation of His promises.

We are commanded in Ephesians 6:2 to honour our parents for there is a promise of long life attached to it. When we honor our parents we carry ourselves well and represent them well. This is how we are to honour our Heavenly Father. When we represent Him well, it glorifies Him.

If we take such measures to ensure that we are honouring our earthly parents, we should do the same or more for our Heavenly Father. Often times we do things because we want to be rewarded, however, most of us love our parents simply because they are our parents, and not for what they can give us. Let's face it, many parents cannot afford to give us what we need, so if we were waiting on that to love them, love would be a long time in coming.

We should love our Heavenly Father simply because of who He is and not because of what He can do for us. Let us love Him for Him and not because of the benefits. Love Him and obey Him just because. *Jesus said, if you love me you will keep my commandments (or my Word).* (John 14:15, 23).

Just as how there is a promise attached to honouring our parents, there are many promises attached to obeying our Heavenly Father. Obedience leads to life. When we honour our earthly parents we are promised long life. Likewise obeying God also leads to life.

The prophet Ezekiel spoke about this. God said through Ezekiel, *They refused to keep my decrees and follow my regulations, even though obedience would have given them life.* (Ezekiel 20:11 NLT).

In Deuteronomy 30:19 (NLT) God gave the Israelites a choice:

Today I have given you a choice between life and death, between blessings and curses. Now I call on Heaven and Earth to witness the choice you make. Oh, that you choose life, so that you and your descendants might live!

Seek first the Kingdom of God and His righteousness. Then everything you need will be given to you.

(Matthew 6:33 NKJV).

Will you honour Him with your life?

70.1 Meditation

References: Psalm 69; Ephesians 6:2; John 14:15, 23; Ezekiel 20:11; Deuteronomy 30:19; Matthew 6:33

1. What stood out for you in this lesson?

2. List some ways in which you honor your earthly parents.

3. How do you honor your Heavenly Father?

4. What promise or promises are associated with:

   a. Honouring our parents?

   b. Honouring God?

5. What should we seek after most, God, His Kingdom, or His benefits? Explain.

6. What does it mean when the scripture says God daily loads us with benefits?

71 Joy Comes in the Morning

I am not a morning person. I am not the one to be bright-eyed and bushy-tailed first thing in the morning. I tend to take it really slow and I am usually good to go by about noon. Some people function best first thing in the morning.

Mornings are a special time of the day. It signifies a brand new day, a new start, a new opportunity to do things differently and it comes with natural light. Darkness departs as the sun rises over the horizon, but will return at its appropriate time. The night and the morning both have their appointed time. The Bible has much to say about morning. King David popularly talks about waking up early in the morning to worship and numerous other scriptures talks about the Israelites worshipping before the Lord early in the morning.

The first reference of morning is in the book of Genesis is when God separated the night from the day, or light from darkness (vv3-4). When we think of light in the spiritual, it has to do with illumination, understanding or revelation. Darkness is the opposite and represents misunderstanding, confusion or ignorance. Darkness flees where light is present. The two are separated and cannot dwell together. Each has its own season and therefore manifests in its time. Each has its purpose – it was in darkness that God called forth light.

This shows me that God is present even in the dark valleys of our lives. He is hovering, waiting for the right time to speak, and when He speaks confusion and ignorance is replaced with revelation and understanding and clarity. In other words darkness flees and light takes its place. We get revelation of what God wants us to do, and receive direction from Him.

KARLENE MILLWOOD

Whatever the situation you are faced with understand that the solution is in your mouth. What are you saying? You have the power to turn it around by speaking what is not as though it were. That is what God did. He spoke the solution to get rid of darkness, darkness fled and "there was light".

In the natural we have the four seasons that dictate our weather; spring, summer, autumn and winter. Darkness and light also have their season that was decided by God at creation. As it is in the natural so it is in the spirit. We all go through different seasons in our lives, but rest assured that the same God that is with us in the morning, is the same God who is present in the night season.

Whenever you are experiencing confusion or misunderstanding about what is happening in your life, know that God is getting ready to move. He is getting ready to do a new thing, to create, to bring about a new season for you.

Sing to the Lord, all you godly ones! Praise His holy name. For His anger lasts only a moment,

But His favour lasts a lifetime! Weeping may last through the night, But joy comes in the morning. (Psalm 30:4-5 NLT).

Dictionary.com defines the word morning as:

1. The first part or period of the day, extending from dawn, or from midnight, to noon
2. The beginning of day; dawn
3. The first or early period of anything

Morning is *the first or early period of anything, or a beginning.* What may God want to do in your life? What new thing may God want to bring about? What have you been praying for?

Behold I will do a new thing, Now it shall spring forth; Shall you not know it? I will even make a road in the wilderness and rivers in the desert. (Isaiah 43:19 NKJV).

If you are in a dark valley right now don't panic. God is present in the darkness, but He doesn't work in darkness. Before God created anything He commanded light. Before He does anything He brings light (understanding, revelation, clarity) first. Continue to seek Him and wait on Him for His revelation. It will come quickly. Speak the word over yourself and speak the solution (what you want to see) to the problem that you are facing.

I remember when I wanted to come out of debt and couldn't see my way out. I didn't have enough money in my savings or checking account so my only other option was to use some of my investments. When I inquired I was told that I couldn't touch some of the money until a specified date, others only at time of retirement, which was years away.

Right there at my desk in the office, I took the word of God to the situation. I brought the situation fully before God and reminded Him of His word in Isaiah 45:2 NIV, which says, *I will go before you and will level the mountains; I will break down gates of bronze and cut through bars of iron.*

I said, "Lord, the bronze gates and iron bars are holding me in and I need them to come down. Thank you for helping me to do this. In Jesus name. Amen."

A series of events transpired over the next couple of weeks which caused that money to be released to me and I was able to pay off all my debts. Oh the joy it brought me to be out from under the weight of debt. I rejoiced and am still rejoicing at the goodness and faithfulness of God.

Weeping may endure for a night, but joy comes in the morning. In light God makes all things new.

In the beginning God created the heavens and the earth. The earth was without form and empty, and darkness covered the deep waters. And the Spirit of God was hovering over the surface of the waters. Then God said, "Let there be light," and there was light. And God saw the light was good. (Genesis 1:1-4a NIV). Then He began to work and the rest is history.

Thank you Lord for the morning. Thank you for the promise of the morning. Morning signifies the end of night and brings with it joy. Thank you for the joyous morning.

71.1 Meditation

References: Genesis 1; Psalm 30:4-5; Isaiah 43:19, 45:2

1. What stood out for you in this lesson?

2. What does the morning represent in the spiritual?

3. What does darkness represent?

4. When you are faced with a problem what should you do?

5. When you declare what you want to see what principle are you activating?

6. Why does the morning bring joy with it?

7. Do you know what spiritual season you are in, in your life?

72 Checkpoint

One night as I was drifting off to sleep I saw a vision of a man being checked at a border. He was heading to Trenton, New Jersey and got stopped at a border point. It was such a clear and specific image that I got up and wrote down what I saw in my journal. Then a question popped into my mind. Why do we get checked before crossing a border into a new place?

Immigration checks us to make sure that our documents are correct and that we are not transporting illegal products or substances across the border. This makes me think of the work of the Holy Spirit in our lives. We cannot go into new spiritual territory, or attain higher heights in the Spirit with illegal stuff. What would qualify as illegal material in the spirit? Anything that is counter to the Spirit of Christ, e.g. bitterness, anger, unforgiveness and so on. To put it bluntly – sin.

As in the natural, you need the right documentation to embark on your spiritual journey. Being born again is your visa into the Kingdom of God and the Holy Spirit is your passport. There are different types of passports and visas and all come with its own privileges e.g. diplomatic, visitor or permanent.

We are likewise awarded certain privileges by the Holy Spirit with each level we go in Him. In order to move to new levels in the Spirit we also have to go through spiritual checkpoints to ensure that we are abiding by the laws of the land (Kingdom of God) before we can go through. We have to purify ourselves of any sin and let go of anything or anyone that could hold us back. We should remove from our lives anything that would slow us down and the sin that so often makes us fall. (Hebrews 12:1b).

KARLENE MILLWOOD

Examine yourself and ask God to reveal anything that would hinder you moving into new territory. Second Corinthians 13:5 encourages us to examine and test ourselves to see if our faith is genuine. You cannot advance in the Spirit if you are still harboring sin in your life. It must be exposed and dealt with. When I say expose, I don't mean you should go confess to the whole congregation. This sort of open confession must be led by the Holy Spirit. I mean acknowledge the sin to God, repent of it and ask His forgiveness.

When you have come to the place where the Holy Spirit checks you and everything is in order, He will move you forward. He alone is the promoter. Let us allow the Holy Spirit to examine us and bring us into right alignment with Him.

72.1 Meditation

References: Hebrews 12:1; 2 Corinthians 13:5

1. What stood out for you in this lesson?

2. What is the purpose of an immigration checkpoint?

3. What equates as an immigration officer in the Spirit?

4. What are the similarities in how the Holy Spirit and an immigration officer works?

5. What would hinder us from passing a checkpoint in the spirit?

6. Is there anything in your life that would hinder you from passing the spiritual checkpoint?

73 Our Refuge and Strength

God is our refuge and strength [mighty and impenetrable to temptation], a very present and well-proved help in trouble. (Psalm 46:1 AMP).

We often speak of the power of God and his unsurpassing strength. But what does it really mean? We understand that because of who He is, there is none stronger and mightier than He. He is the Almighty God. But what does that strength look like? How can we put it in perspective to truly understand His greatness?

Let's break out each of these words and examine their meaning.

Mighty: Characterized by, or showing superior power and strength.
Great in importance. Exceptional.

Impenetrable: Cannot be penetrated, pierced or entered.
Inaccessible to ideas and influences.
Incapable of being understood, unfathomable.

Temptation: Enticement, allurement especially to evil.

Throughout scripture God is referred to as mighty, or a Mighty Warrior. His strength and power is unsurpassed by any human and He is the only true and living God, so there is not another in the God class that can be compared to Him. He is God all by Himself. He is impenetrable to temptation. That means He cannot ever succumb to temptation in any form, because He is not influenced at all by outside opinions.

God is a King and He has a Kingdom. He makes the rules for His Kingdom and no one can undo them. Humanity may choose to ignore them, or try to bring them down to their level, but it doesn't make God's rules obsolete or ineffective. He sits as King forever. (Psalm 10:16, 29:10). No one put Him on His throne and no one can remove Him. So whether or not humanity chooses to acknowledge Him, He remains firmly seated over all creation as Creator King.

Many earthly Kingdoms have risen and fallen throughout history. We read of great conquerors like Hannibal Barca of the North African Empire of Carthage who was known as probably the greatest military strategist that ever lived.

Then there were Alexander the Great, Napoleon Bonaparte and so many others that we can name. Yet, in all their greatness, none of them could compare to God in His might and power. They were powerful rulers that reigned over large Kingdoms, but where are those Kingdoms today? Our God is the greatest of all!

King David trusted God in all his battles and God gave him the victory. He led Joshua to topple the city of Jericho and to defeat the five evil Kings. Before that He brought Egypt to its knees with the plagues through Moses, and Gideon defeated the Midianites with only 300 men.

No matter what situation you are facing God knows how to get you through. His thoughts are higher than our thoughts, and his ways are higher than our ways. (Isaiah 55:8 KJV). Find your strength in Him.

Yes! God's riches are very great! His wisdom and knowledge have no end! No one can explain what God decides. No one can understand his ways. As the scriptures say, "Who can know what is on the Lord's mind? Who is able to give him advice?" (Romans 11:33-34 ESV). One scripture asks, is there anything too hard for God?

He is with you in the midst of the trouble so be comforted that you are not walking through it alone. He promises never to leave us or forsake us. David was well aware of the Lord's presence in his dark moments when he penned the twenty-third Psalm. He said, *"Yeah though I walk through the valley of the shadow of death I will fear no evil for thou art with me."* (Psalm 23:4 KJV).

Do you believe that the Almighty, impenetrable, exceptional God is with you and for you? Then why worry? He has already made a way of escape out of your situation. Just trust Him and know that nothing that comes against Him or His Kingdom can ever succeed. His Kingdom will last forever and you are a part of it. He has a well-proven track record.

Well-proved: Establish truth or genuineness by evidence or argument. Establish authenticity or validity.
To demonstrate by action. To test to determine quality, character etc.
To show oneself to have the character or ability expected of one, through one's actions.

How do we test God to prove Him?

We do it by exercising our faith. First we have to know what the promises are concerning the situation or circumstance, then employ our faith, based on that word. How do we know that God is faithful, or that His word is true if we don't put Him to the test? I have mentioned elsewhere in this book, several times when I trusted God and saw Him come through for me.

If you can't find your own faith, then draw on His well-proved track record with Joshua, Moses, Gideon, Deborah, Samuel, and the list goes on. Put your God to the test everyday by taking Him at His word.

Let us hold tightly without wavering to the hope we affirm, for God can be trusted to keep his promise. (Hebrews 10:23 NLT).

23.1 Meditation

References: Psalm10:16, 29:10, 23:4, 46:1; Isaiah 55:8; Romans 11:33-34; Hebrews 10:23

1. What stood out for you in this lesson?

2. When we say God is Mighty, what does it mean?

3. In your own words, explain God's Kingship and His Kingdom. Use scriptures.

4. When we are in trouble, who is God to us?

5. List some times when we saw God's might in scriptures?

6. How can we prove that God is who He says He is?

74 Worship

I was singing a chorus in worship to the Lord one morning. As I sang I lifted my hands up to Heaven. When I did I got a very clear image of Nazi Germany and of people lifting their hands to salute Adolf Hitler. I was so shocked that I would see that image in a time of worship, but it was for a reason.

The Holy Spirit imparted to me that the way I lift my hands in worship to Him, is the way the Arian nation used to lift their hand to worship Hitler. This was very interesting to me. Suffice it say, the Holy Spirit confirmed it later that night through our pastor in Bible study.

In the gospel of John chapter four verses twenty-one to twenty-four, Jesus has a discourse with the Samaritan woman about worship. Now here was Jesus breaking all social conventions by even interacting with this woman. Jews and Samaritans did not get along during those times, plus it was not socially acceptable for a man to engage a woman in conversation when she was alone.

Jesus cut through all the red tape and got down to the heart of the matter. He was more interested in ministering to a broken soul than in following social norms. He says to her in verse twenty-two (NLT), *"You Samaritans know very little about the one you worship, while we Jews know all about Him, for salvation comes through the Jews."*

Hold up. Stop. Pause. Do you see what I see? Reading in context from verse twenty one, these four verses speak volumes to me. They tell me:

- It is possible to worship someone or something that we don't know.
- It is possible to be ignorant of why we worship.
- There is a right and a wrong way to worship.
- Going to a particular place to worship can become ritualistic as a result of the preceding three points.
- There are true and false worshippers.
- Worship is geared toward or dedicated to something or someone.

Wow! Interesting huh?

If we don't know who, what or why we worship, then our worship is vain. We might as well be worshipping Hitler. When we go through the motions of worship, without understanding what we are doing, or why we are doing it, worship becomes religious ritual. The right way to worship is to first know who we are worshipping and the criteria for worshipping that being.

If we don't know what is required of us during worship, we approach it with the wrong mindset, abuse the practice and fail to experience the benefits. That type of worship is ineffective. We no longer have to wait until we get to a church building to worship. We need to change the mindset that we are going to church, and realize that we are the church. That means we worship wherever we are: home, office, church building, school, wherever.

It is not the place that is important, it's the heart posture. What or who am I focused on during worship? Corporate worship is necessary according to scripture but it does not have to be in a building. It could be in a park or other outdoor location.

True worshippers allow the Holy Spirit to lead them in worship. They are guided by the Spirit and they speak the truth about who He is. False worshippers go through ritual. They worship with unclean hearts so their worship is dedicated to idols and insincere.

The Psalmist said it best in chapter 24. *Who may climb the mountain of the Lord? Who may stand in His holy place? Only those whose hands and hearts are pure, who do not worship idols and never tell lies (Psalm 24:3-4 NLT).*

Who is your mind focused on during worship? Whatever you set your mind on becomes your God. Ask the Holy Spirit to help you to keep your mind on Him.

KARLENE MILLWOOD

74.1 Meditation

References: John 4:21-24; Psalm 24:3-4

1. What stood out for you in this lesson?

2. What is the purpose of worship?

3. Why do we worship?

4. When is worship vain?

5. What role does your mind play in worship?

6. What is the difference between a true worshipper and a false worshipper?

7. Which one are you?

75 Exuberant Praise

I *will praise you, Lord my God, with all my heart; I will glorify your name forever.* (Psalm 86:12 NKJV).

Come, let us sing to the Lord! Let us shout joyfully to the Rock of our salvation. (Psalm 95:1 NKJV).

The Bible is full of verses telling us to praise God. The word praise, and its variations, are mentioned in the King James Version of the Bible approximately 314 times. That's one time for almost every day of the year.[7]

There are seven Hebrew words for praise[8]:

1. Halal – from which we get the word hallelujah
   Meaning: to shine, to boast, celebrate, to be clamorously foolish
   (Psalm 113:1-3, 150:1; 149:3)

2. Yadah
   Meaning: to extend the hand in worship
   (Psalm 63:1; 107:15; 2 Chronicles 20:21)

3. Towdah – From the same root word as Yadah
   Meaning: Lifting of the hands in thanksgiving for things not yet received
   (Psalm 50:14, 23; Jeremiah 33:11; 2 Chronicles 29:31)

---

[7] Google.com

[8] http://buddysheets.tripod.com/hebrewwordsforpraise.htm

KARLENE MILLWOOD

4. Shabach
   Meaning: To shout triumphantly
   (Psalm 47:1; 145:4; Isaiah 12:6)

5. Barak
   Meaning: To kneel and bless God in adoration
   (Psalm 95:6, 34:1; 1 Chronicles 29:20)

6. Zamar
   Meaning: to praise with joyful singing and music accompanied by instruments
   (Psalm 21:13, 57:8-9; 1 Chronicles 16:9)

7. Tehillah – from Halal
   Meaning: to sing or laud with music
   (Psalm 22:3, 33:1; Isaiah 61:3)

Each of these words describe an act (a manner) in which we praise God.

I came to a point of worship at home one evening where I saw (in the Spirit) an image of Jesus coming into the room and standing in front of me. My hands were lifted up in that moment of worship and for a second, I felt like I could reach out and touch Him physically. It was such an amazing and surreal feeling. I was reminded in that moment that when we praise we build a highway for Him to come and inhabit our praise (Psalm 22:3). What an awesome manifestation of that scripture! What an awesome manifestation of the Presence of God showing up!

To quote Dr. Myles Munroe, "God's presence is conditional. He doesn't come simply because we want Him to. He comes when the conditions are right." I think the conditions were right for Him that day and He showed up in person. To God be the glory.

Praise is important in the Kingdom of God. It is how we show our appreciation to our Heavenly Father for His goodness, faithfulness, kindness and patience to us and with us. I asked myself the question, why do I praise? Do I praise simply because everybody around me is praising in a church service? Or do I have a genuine reason for my praise?

Oh yes I do. My praise is genuine and arises out of gratitude for who God is in my life. When I think about how good God has been to me, I praise

Him. When I remember the things He brought me through and delivered me from, I praise Him. When I think of the numerous times He healed my body, I praise Him. I have numerous reasons to be grateful to Him and I express that gratefulness through praise.

Not only do I praise Him for what He has done for me, I praise Him just because of who He is. The songwriter wrote, "Because of who you are I give you glory, because of who you are I give you praise. Because of who you are, I lift my voice in praise. Lord I worship you because of who you are."

She then continues by listing some of His titles – Jehovah Jireh, our provider. Jehovah Nissi, our Lord of victory and so on. Each of these tells of a characteristic of God and speaks of ways in which He works in our lives. He is El-Shaddai, the many breasted One. That means He can be to you whatever or whoever you need Him to be.

King David said, *"My soul shall make her boast in the Lord."* (Psalm 34:2 KJV). Because of who we were when God chose us, the Apostle Paul tells us that we have no right to boast (of ourselves) in His presence. All the glory goes to Him. If all the glory is God's then we are to boast about Him – His goodness, attributes, and his promises, and we do that in and through our praise.

I love to listen to jazz and one of my favourite jazz artistes is Kirk Whalum, a brother in Christ. He does these wonderful compilations titled, The Gospel According to Jazz, where he uses his musical gift to glorify God. He has a song on the first installment of the series called In All the Earth.

It is a joyful, jazzy rendition of praise to the Most High God. I mention it here because it is playing in the background as I write.

In all the earth, let the name of the Lord be praised

In all the earth, let the standard of His holiness be raised

O Lord our Lord how majestic is thy name…

A truly beautiful rendition of praise to God. What are your reasons for praising God? I encourage you to incorporate exuberant praise in your daily activities.

25.1 Meditation

References: Psalm 21:13, 22:3, 33:1, 34:1, 47:1, 50:14, 57:8-9, 63:1, 95:6, 107: 15, 113:1-3, 150:1; 145:4, 149:3,; 1 Chronicles 16:9, 29:20; 2 Chronicles 20:21; 23; 29:31; Isaiah 12:6, 61:3; Jeremiah 33:11

1. What stood out for you in this lesson?

2. How many ways can we praise God?

3. When we praise, what happens in the spirit?

4. How many times does the word praise occur in the Bible?

5. Why do we praise God?

6. What are some of the benefits of our praise?

76 Conclusion

From a young age, many of us were told that if we get saved we will go to Heaven and if we don't we will go to hell. As a result many of us accepted Christ as Lord and Saviour simply to avoid going to hell. The thought of going to hell terrorized me as a child and so at the tender age of ten, I gave my life to Jesus, not understanding the implications of that bold and life-changing step.

It was no surprise then, that later in my early adult years, I walked away from the church and started doing my own thing. I found out quickly that you can't outrun God once He has a hold of your heart. Life wasn't all I thought it would be and I ran into many situations that made me miserable and led to me feeling incomplete. With every situation I realized that there was a deep longing for something more. I wasn't sure what the more was, I just knew I needed more.

I had tried several other options, including considering different religions, by the time I decided to renew my walk with Christ. When I made that decision I knew in that moment that there was no turning back anymore and it has been an interesting and enlightening journey up until now. I hear many stories from different people of how they came to Christ, and listened to the testimonies of how He has worked in their lives.

The preceding chapters are a few testimonies of my personal walk as I learn and grow in the grace and knowledge of our Lord and Saviour, Jesus Christ. When I share my testimonies in different forums, men and women usually comment on how my words encourage them. My purpose for compiling these devotionals was to speak to women in whatever capacity they function. I spoke to mothers, worship leaders, gardeners, career

KARLENE MILLWOOD

professionals and more. I hope you were all equally blessed by the insights in this book.

I hope you will be inspired to read the chapters over and over again and glean more wisdom and new revelations from them every time.

Yours in Christ.

References

Moore, Beth (2011) So Long Insecurity, Tyndale House Publishing.

Meyer, Joyce (2002) Battlefield of the Mind. Revised Edition. Warner Faith Publishing.

Munroe, Myles (2000) The Purpose and Power of Praise and Worship. Destiny Image Publishers.

Munroe, Myles (date unknown) How to Walk in Confidence [online]. Available at: https://www.youtube.com/watch?v=53ZtnvjPeXE. Accessed: June 27, 2016.

Bevere, Lisa (2016) Without Rival. Revell: Baker Publishing Group.

Liardon, R. (1996) God's Generals: Why They Succeeded and Why Some Failed, 4th Edition. Albury Publishing.

Thoele, S.P. (2003) The Woman's Book of Courage. Conari Press.

Hillman, Os (2015) TGIF2: His Vision. His Way. His Timing. [online]. Available at: www.TodayGodIsFirst.com. Accessed: October 27, 2015

Hillman-Brown. C. (2016) TGIF Next Gen: Dealing with Frustrations [online]. Prism Ministries. Available at: https://www.prismministries.org. Accessed: March 5, 2016.

Hillman-Brown. C. (2016) TGIF Next Gen: The Safe Way [online]. Prism Ministries. Available at: https://www.prismministries.org. Accessed: Aug. 24, 2016.

Trimm, C. (2016) Faith to Faith [online]. Available at: https://www.youtube.com/watch?v=6c_2Hpt5VTw. Accessed: August 4, 2016.

Trimm, C. (2016) Destiny Decisions [online]. Available at: https://www.youtube.com/watch?v=6zbV-zWaTL4. Accessed: August29, 2016.

Trimm, C. (2010) The Art of War for Spiritual Battles: Essential Tactics and Strategies for Spiritual Warfare. Charisma House.

Hobbs, Dianna (2016) Empowering Everyday Women [online]. Available at: https://www.diannahobbs.com. Accessed: Varied.

Author unknown (date unknown) Hebrew Words of Praise [online]. Available at: http://buddysheets.tripod.com/hebrewwordsforpraise.htm. Accessed: Dec. 15, 2016.

Helpguide. Org (2016) Effective Communication. [online]. Available at: https://www.helpguide.org/articles/relationships/effective-communication.htm. Accessed: Nov. 10, 2016.

Arborday.org (2016) Tree Life Stages. [online]. Available at: https://www.arborday.org/trees/lifestages/ Accessed: April 26, 2014.

CSLI (2006) Reflections – Thoughts for The Journey. [online]. Available at: http://www.cslewisinstitute.org/webfm_send/115. Accessed: February 13, 2017.

Lewis, C.S. (unknown) Quote. [online]. Available at: http://www.goodreads.com/quotes/110054-the-more-we-let-god-take-us-over-the-more. Accessed: February 13, 2017.

Allen, James (2007) As A Man Thinketh. 1st Edition. Dover Publications.

The Author

Karlene Millwood is an entrepreneur, poet, author, playwright and screenwriter. When she is not in Ontario, Canada, where she resides, she is off discovering unique and interesting places and people to write about.

She gives God thanks for her wonderful life, and the beautiful gift of His continuous presence.

To invite Karlene to speak at your event, send an email to info@jazzdvineent.com.

A Bucket Full of
Mangoes
A Collection of Sweet Stories for
the Entire Family

by Karlene Millwood

Other Books by This Author

T he collection of short stories is a touching and humorous recount of life in the Caribbean island of Jamaica. Told through the eyes of a young Kerri-Ann, readers are given a rare glimpse of the strong family values and vibrant culture, of a country noted for producing some of the world's greatest artists, civil rights leaders and athletes.

Printed in the United States
By Bookmasters